Signs of the Times

by Allan Walker, Ph.D.

Signs of the Times

© 2018 Allan Walker

Self-Published on KDP

(Amazon Kindle Direct Publishing)

www.awmin.org

For permission, contact:

Allan Walker Ministries
P.O. Box 94
Nowata, OK 74048
awm@awmin.org

Although the author and the editor have made every effort to ensure the accuracy and completeness of information contained in this book, we assume no responsibilities for errors, inaccuracies, omissions, or any inconsistency herein.

The external website addresses included in any part of this book are offered as a resource. These websites are not intended in any way to be or imply an endorsement on the part of Allan Walker Ministries, nor do we vouch for their content.

Edited by Beth Ann Luebke.

ISBN 978-1-7241-0253-9 (KDP)

Published in the United States, 2018.

Table of Contents

Chapter 1

The Divine Design of Bible Prophecy

A s the Lord Jesus Christ ascended back into heaven His disciples gazed intently upon Him. The angel told them, "This same Jesus who is taken from you shall so come in like manner as you have seen Him go." The promises for the return of Christ are repeated throughout the New Testament writings and constitute a major doctrine in scripture.

The prophecies of the seventieth week of Daniel are generally believed to coincide with chapters 6-19 in the book of Revelation. This seven-year period will consummate God's dealings with unbelieving Israel, bringing them to national repentance and usher in the millennial reign of the Messiah.

While the rapture of the church is imminent, the signs of the end of the age indicate that both Daniel's Seventieth week and Christ's second coming are approaching. No signs must be fulfilled before the rapture takes place.

Dr. J. Dwight Pentecost states:

> Such passages as 1 Thessalonians 5:6; Titus 2:13; Revelation 3:3 all warn the believer to be watching for the Lord Himself, not for signs that would precede His coming. It is true that the events of the seventieth week will cast an adumbration before the rapture, but the object of the believer's attention is always directed to Christ, never to these portents.[1]

We have seen decades of widespread interest in current events and Bible prophecy, especially since Hal Lindsey wrote *The Late Great Planet Earth* in 1970.

This book:

> became one of the best-selling works of non-fiction in that decade. It was published in 54 languages and has sold approximately 35 million copies. *Late Great* talks about the

undeniable signs of the end times: the rebirth of Israel, war in the Middle East, natural disasters, the revival of Satanism and witchcraft and many others. These were prophesied long ago by prophets from Moses to Jesus and tell of a soon-coming antichrist and the destruction of the world as we know it. But the true purpose of this book is to bring a message of hope and a future to throngs of desperate, dying people. Successful at its main purpose, this book has been used to bring over a million souls to Christ.[2]

The late Dr. Tim LaHaye co-authored the phenomenal *Left Behind* fiction series with Jerry B. Jenkins, between 1995 and 2007. This series:

has broken all publishing records with a total of 80 million in print. These books have appeared on the best-seller lists of The New York Times, USA Today, Wall Street Journal, Publishers Weekly, and Christian Booksellers Association. Based on the Bible's book of Revelation, the apocalyptic thrillers follow the lives of those left behind after the sudden disappearance of millions of believers.[3]

The generation following the restoration of Israel has seen a precise pattern of events come to pass, just as prophesied in the Scriptures centuries ago. While the church is watching and waiting for the imminent return of Christ, it is clear that current events are setting the stage for Daniel's Seventieth Week. *Time Magazine* featured as their cover article, "The Bible and the Apocalypse: Why more Americans are reading and talking about the end of the World" in July 2002.

Many books have outlined these prophecies; however, the details of prophecy are amplified and much better understood using charts or other visual aids. Clarence Larkin was a pioneer in this area, using his background as a professional draftsman, to teach prophecy using charts. His charts were published in 1918 in the book, Dispensational Truth.[4] Others have created a variety of prophetic charts since that time. In 1969, Leon Bates published "A Bible Map" followed by the publication of "The Tribulation Map," in 1974. These two charts have been used worldwide since that time. The Bible Map and Tribulation Map outline God's order of events for the ages in an easy to understand visual format. They are illustrated on the next pages.

Many evangelicals follow a literal, grammatical interpretation of the study of Bible prophecy, referred to as premillennial dispensationalism. This school of interpretation teaches that God has segmented all of human history into seven distinct dispensations or time periods. God deals differently with various people groups in each dispensation. We are now living in dispensation six, which will close with the rapture of the church. This is followed by a seven-year tribulation period, climaxing with the literal, visible return of Christ to set up His kingdom and reign on Earth for one thousand years, which will be the seventh dispensation.

Dr. Pentecost noted the scope and importance of Bible prophecy:

> Biblical Eschatology is the capstone of systematic theology. It is not only climactic, the terminus and consummation of theological study, but the presentation of eschatology is also the supreme demonstration of theological skill.[5]

Dispensationalists believe history will be consummated just as the scriptures have literally foretold. While many sensational and even foolish speculations have brought reproach on the subject of prophecy, it still stands as some of the strongest evidence for the supernatural character and divine inspiration of the Holy Scriptures. When the prophecies of scripture are compared with the major news events of our time, there is substantial evidence that we are living near the end of the age.

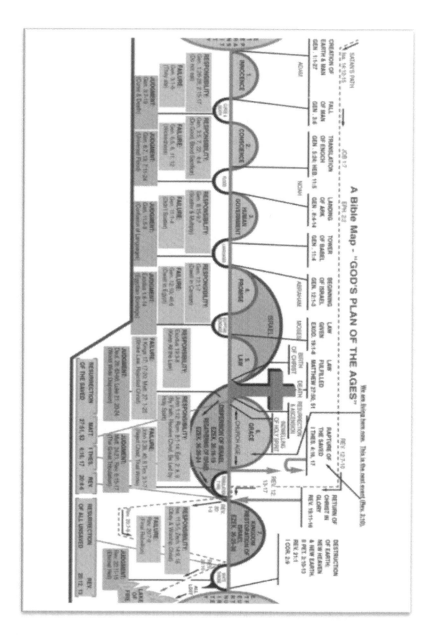

Chart 1: Bates, "A Bible Map," The Bible Believers Evangelistic Association. https://bbea.org/

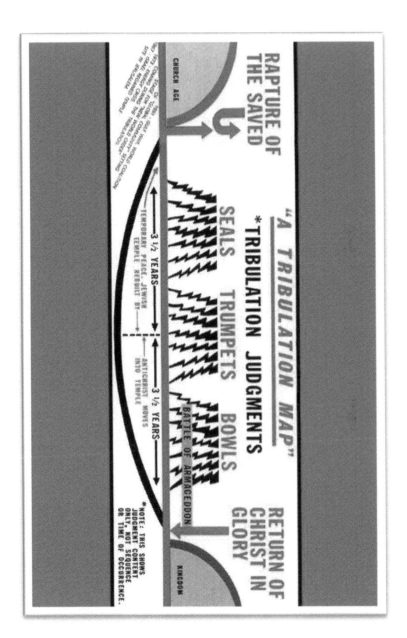

Chart 2: Bates, "A Tribulation Map," The Bible Believers Evangelistic Association. https://bbea.org/

Chapter 2

Sign One: Ancient Prophecies Coming into Focus

While the coming of Christ has been imminent since the days of the Apostles, scripture indicates there will be specific characteristics of the generation which will appear near the return of Christ for His church. Israel was scattered among the nations in A.D. 70 and was temporarily set aside in the plan of God. God has been visiting the Gentile nations to call out a people for His name. Any individual Jew or Gentile can respond to the gospel message and become part of the body of Christ. God will resume His dealings with national Israel only after the church age is completed. Israel is the primary focus of the apocalyptic events in Revelation 6-19; although they will be experienced worldwide. Near the end of the seven-year tribulation, Israel will be facing annihilation, and it is at that point that Jesus Christ intervenes and is revealed to them as their Messiah. A remnant will be converted to Christ and meet the Lord at His second advent when He rescues them from pending destruction.

Are there any good reasons to believe our time is different from any other in history and we might be the generation to see the return of Christ? Consider these:

For the first time in history, man has the capacity to:

- Destroy all life on planet Earth (Matt. 24:21-22)
- Destroy one half of humanity in the tribulation (Rev. 6:8; 9:15)
- Burn one-third of the earth by fire (Rev. 9:18)
- Generate 100-pound hailstones with nuclear weapons (Rev. 16:21)
- Cause human flesh to melt from the body instantly (Zech. 14:12)
- Number and track the buying and selling of all mankind (Rev.13:16-18)
- Address all mankind and broadcast any event to a global audience (Rev. 11:7-12)

Certain key events are predicted for the last days:

- The Information Age: an increase in knowledge and travel (Dan. 12:4)
- Widespread persecution and martyrdom of Christians (Matt. 10:22; Rev. 6:9)
- A revival of ancient occultism and eastern mysticism (Matt. 24:5)
- A widespread interest in UFOs and extraterrestrial beings (2 Thess. 2:11-12)
- A global outpouring of The Holy Spirit with preaching of the Gospel (Acts 2:16-18)
- The rise of many false Christs and false prophets who work miracles (Matt. 24:5)
- Rejection of biblical authority and doctrine by false church leaders (1 Tim. 4:1; Rev. 17)
- Many depart from the faith and give heed to seducing spirits (1 Tim. 4:1-6)
- An ecumenical movement emerges uniting all religions into a false church (Rev. 17)
- Widespread unbelief in the Rapture and the Second Coming of Christ (2 Pet. 3:3-4)

The nations of the world aligned in Bible prophecy:

- Israel is restored as a nation after a 2000-year dispersion (Ezek. 37:39)
- Jerusalem becomes a burdensome political problem to world leaders (Zech. 12:3)
- The Arab-Israeli conflict over land and the city of Jerusalem (Gen. 17:20-21; Rev. 6-19)
- Europe is united as a superpower with a movement for world government (Dan. 2:37-44)
- There is a call for one man to lead the entire world (Rev. 13:8)

- Hatred of the Islamic nations for the reborn state of Israel (Gen. 16:11-13)
- Russia and her Islamic allies invade Israel during the tribulation period (Ezek. 1 38-39)
- China and her Oriental allies move into the Middle East (Rev.16:12-14)
- The USA and her allies are drawn into the Arab-Israeli conflict (Ezek. 38-39; Rev. 6-19)
- The Arab-Israeli conflict involves all the nations of the world (Ezek. 38-39; Rev. 6-19)
- Armageddon threatens the survival of the human race (Matt. 24:21-22)
- The return of Christ to Earth saves mankind from complete annihilation (Rev. 19:11-16)

The twentieth century saw the restoration of Israel as a nation in 1948 and their recovery of Jerusalem in 1967. Israel is surrounded by hostile Islamic enemies who are intent upon her destruction. The United States, the European Union, Russia and China each have an interest in the outcome of this conflict. An ongoing international conflict continues which world leaders are unable to solve. Seventy years after the restoration of Israel, it remains the focal issue in world affairs. The Middle East dominates the news and world leaders do not have a permanent solution for it. It is this precise scenario that was predicted by the biblical prophets 2,700 years ago.

From this list of prophecies, it is obvious to even the casual reader that world affairs and Bible prophecy have merged together with uncanny precision. We will look at each of these and see how they fit into the big picture.

For the first time in history, it is possible to destroy all life on planet Earth. To the skeptic who doubts that a sovereign God could bring this about, we can say that mankind has the capacity to do this with nuclear weapons. If God allowed that to happen, humanity would be destroyed. Through decades of ministry Dr.

Billy Graham always emphasized that God would not allow the human race to destroy itself, but He would send Jesus Christ back to Earth to set up His kingdom and rescue man from his own devices.

Although God will not allow the total annihilation of humanity, scripture prophesies that half of humanity will be killed during the tribulation period. Even secular analysts are aware of the dangers facing mankind as rogue nations acquire chemical, biological and nuclear weapons. Many of these nations are motivated by radical Islam, Communism or other ideologies, which place little value on human life. There are prophetic analysts who believe all these judgments will be sovereign acts of God, while others suggest God lifts His restraining hand and allows man to bring these judgments on himself. Either way, they are literally fulfilled.

Scripture prophesies that one-third of the earth will be burned by fire. It is difficult to imagine the magnitude of nuclear weapons many times more powerful than those used at Hiroshima and Nagasaki. With many of these detonated in close proximity to each other, it is not difficult to envision one-third of the earth burned by fire as the nations mentioned in prophecy are drawn into a nuclear holocaust over Israel and Jerusalem.

Scripture speaks of 100-pound hailstones falling in Revelation 16:21. When the USA tested nuclear weapons in the Marshall Islands in 1946, moisture was driven into the stratosphere where it is some 70°F below zero. The blasts generated chunks of ice that fell back down to earth and dented aircraft carriers in the area. To the skeptic who questions that God could or would rain down 100-pound hailstones, it is clear that man can do this with modern technology.

Scripture speaks of a man's flesh melting from his skeleton while he stands on his feet. Some nuclear weapons generate a temperature of 10 million degrees. This is the first time in history that mankind has developed the technology which can literally fulfill this prophecy. These first five points all are the result of nuclear weapons, unique to this generation.

Scripture indicates that the Antichrist will implement a mark where no man can buy or sell unless he has a number. Our computerized banking system makes it possible to track all banking and commerce electronically. Records exist of where a person was, what they purchased, how much they spent, and what their credit line was. Closely related are cell phone records with one's actual location and personal contacts. Internet history reveals the online activity of users whether for business, political, religious or personal interests. Peter Lalonde once asked, "Is Big Brother watching you? He then said, "Probably not, but he could be if he wanted to."

Scripture speaks of the two witnesses being killed by the Antichrist. Their dead bodies will lie in the streets of Jerusalem and the entire world will see it occur. When the Antichrist goes into the temple and proclaims himself to be God, there is no doubt the major news networks will beam his message to a global audience through satellite television. Surely, the media will be a factor in his rise to power. That same technology is currently being used to preach the gospel of Jesus Christ to the world. The media can be used for good or evil purposes.

The information age:

So much information is available to us that we must carefully decide what to use and what to discard. Supersonic jets make it possible to be on the other side of the world in a matter of hours. Scripture prophesies that knowledge and travel will increase in the last days

Consider the following:

> On average human knowledge is doubling every 13 months. According to IBM, the buildout of the "internet of things" will lead to the doubling of knowledge every 12 hours.[1]

Widespread persecution and martyrdom of Christians is prophesied for the tribulation period:

We are seeing an alarming rise in persecution even now. More Christians were killed for their faith in the 20th century than in all previous centuries combined, and this has been reported by numerous groups. The Voice of the Martyrs[1] is one ministry that now works in 68 countries where Christians are persecuted for spreading the gospel. In Islamic, Communist, Buddhist and Hindu nations, many governments are either persecuting believers or do not provide the protection they need.

Hillary Clinton, in the 2016 election campaign, mentioned Christian persecution as a key international issue. Clinton called ISIS atrocities against Christians "genocide" in response to a question from a New Hampshire voter in December. More recently, Trump outlined atrocities against Christians, calling for an end to the "campaign of absolute and total genocide" by ISIS when he unveiled his anti-terrorism plan in August."[2]

The twentieth century has seen a revival of occult practices and New Age mysticism:

> In 1979, *Time* magazine estimated some 40,000 witches were active in the United States. Today, the figure may have quadrupled, with an equal number of Satanists; regardless, over 300 universities, colleges, and educational institutions (over 75 are accredited or state-approved) now offer programs or even degrees on New Age topics; some 100 American universities also offer courses in witchcraft, and in Britain alone, today, there are an estimated 50,000 to 75,000 [spiritualists] plus 40,000 to 100,000 witches and Satanists. Forty years ago, all this was unheard of.[3]

There is no question that these current trends will continue throughout this age. The spirit of Antichrist is in the world today

---

[1] *For more information about The Voice of the Martyrs visit www.persecution.com*

and will lead to the revelation of the Antichrist in the tribulation period. The stage is even now being set for the delusion of that time.

Widespread interest in UFOs and Extraterrestrial beings:

Closely related to the revival of occult practices is a growing interest in UFO sightings and belief in extra-terrestrial beings. While many evangelical Christians do not believe in ETs or UFOs as presented by science fiction, UFO consciousness exists in society today.

According to a *National Geographic* survey: "77 percent of all Americans believes there are signs that aliens have visited Earth" and according to a recent Harris poll only 68 percent of all Americans believe that Jesus is God or the Son of God. That means that the number of Americans that believe that UFOs have visited us is now greater than the number of Americans that believe what the Bible has to say about Jesus Christ. With each passing year, the frequency of UFO sightings seems to keep increasing, as does the number of movies, television shows and video games featuring aliens and extraterrestrial life. It is almost as if the population of the planet is being primed for something. Could this phenomenon be the "strong delusion" of the last days that is talked about in the Bible? And if there are beings out there that are not human, what is it that they want? Could it be that they have an extremely insidious agenda?

When it comes to UFOs, it is important to be skeptical. These days it is very easy to fake just about anything on video, and there have definitely been a lot of fraudulent reports over the years.

But virtually all of those that have studied this phenomenon for many years come away convinced that something very unusual is clearly happening in our skies. Every year there are hundreds upon hundreds of very credible reports of very strange unidentified flying objects that seem to have no natural explanation.[4]

A global outpouring of The Holy Spirit with worldwide preaching of the gospel:

According to the National Light for the Lost Director of The Assemblies of God, "70 percent of all evangelism ever done has been since 1900, 75 percent of that has been done since World War II and 70 percent of that has been done in the last 36 months."[5]

It is difficult to number believers from Pentecostal and Charismatic churches. Those who have written on the topic say that there are

> Analysts estimate that two-thirds of the approximately 100 million or more Christians in China are Pentecostal. Brazil alone has almost 23 million Assemblies of God believers, and South Korea has more than 3 million.
>
> In the last decade, the world population grew 1.2 percent and the Christian population grew at almost exactly the same rate. Evangelical population growth more than doubled at 2.5 percent. The Assemblies of God average annual growth rate for the decade was 4 percent. Such huge numbers of Spirit-filled believers in the world today are the result of fervent missions and evangelism, as Pentecostals obeyed Jesus' commands to proclaim the gospel and make disciples in the entire world."[6]

To further emphasize the outpouring of the Spirit, the Hartford Institute explains:

> In 2011, there were an estimated 584 million Pentecostal and Charismatic Christians worldwide. They made up 8.5 percent of the world's population and 27 percent of all Christians. There were 279 million Pentecostals and over

300 million Charismatics (the figures for Charismatics include both the Charismatic Movement in the historic churches as well as the neo-charismatic movement). Pentecostal and Charismatic Christianity is second in size only to the Roman Catholic Church.

New research shows 50 percent more megachurches in the United States than previously thought.

They further add:

Initial analysis of a cooperative project to survey all megachurches in the United States by Scott Thumma of Hartford Seminary's Hartford Institute for Religion Research, and Dave Travis and Warren Bird of Leadership Network uncovered at least 1,200 Protestant churches that claim more than 2,000 weekly worship attenders.

This figure is nearly 50 percent more than the figure of 850 commonly assumed and quoted by both organizations and other researchers of very large churches.

"I would never have guessed that either of our groups could have missed so many additional megachurches," said Thumma, a professor of sociology at Hartford Seminary who specializes in the study of such churches.

Many of the new congregations were uncovered when the two groups, which both keep separate lists of megachurches, compared their records. Each group knew of different sets of congregations, with the two lists overlapping on about 600 churches. It was the names of those that did not overlap that pushed the total list to just over the 1,200 mark.

"Our preliminary research for the major survey effort indicates there could very well be another 200 to 400 megachurches in addition to these," Bird said. "We'll have to see what information the questionnaires return to know for sure." [7]

In an article by The Pew Forum, the numbers of Christians continue to show extraordinary growth.

The number of Christians around the world has nearly quadrupled in the last 100 years, from about 600 million in 1910 to more than 2 billion in 2010. But the world's overall population also has risen rapidly, from an estimated 1.8 billion in 1910 to 6.9 billion in 2010. As a result, Christians make up about the same portion of the world's population today (32 percent) as they did a century ago (35 percent)"[8]

Some dispensational prophecy teachers have an excessive emphasis on predestination and ultra-dispensationalism. When coupling excesses of those teachings with an overemphasis on last day's apostasy; little, if any room is left for a significant evangelistic revival during the dispensation of grace. The missionary movement is the heartbeat of God!

Many in the modern mission's movement have an aversion toward the dispensational view of Bible prophecy. Many ultra-dispensationalists have unnecessarily limited the plan of God and leave no room for an outpouring of the Holy Spirit and any measure of success in world evangelism. It is tragic that two very large circles in the church who agree on the fundamentals of the faith are divided on two important issues in the plan of God, world evangelism and teaching of God's prophetic plan. Satan must be delighted!

The late Dr. David Allen Lewis once asked the question, "Will there be revival or apostasy in the last days?" His simple, yet direct answer was: YES! A balanced view of God's plan will acknowledge both scriptural concepts.

The rise of many false Christs and false prophets who work miracles:

The twentieth century has seen a heightened interest in the supernatural, both in the church and in the world. In 1974, Hal Lindsey authored, *Satan is Alive and Well on Planet Earth,* documenting this "occult revival." New Age mysticism is widespread in our culture yet today. One of the key New Age beliefs is that we are all Christ's in various degrees. A typical New Age quote is, "Jesus was 'A' Christ, but you are 'A' Christ and I am 'A' Christ; we are ALL Christs." This contradicts the biblical teaching that Jesus Christ is God incarnate, the unique Son of God, and the judge of all mankind. Even among the church, many are moving into extreme heresy and open apostasy, yet drawing away many followers after themselves. Some who purport to work miracles have been exposed as frauds and charlatans. Jesus was very clear in the Sermon on the Mount when He said,

> Not everyone that saith unto me Lord, Lord, will enter into the Kingdom of Heaven; but he that doeth the will of my Father which is in heaven. Many will say to me in that day, "Lord, Lord, have we not prophesied in thy name? and in thy name have cast out devils? and in thy name done many wonderful works?" And then will I profess unto them, I never knew you: depart from me ye that work iniquity. (Matt. 7:21-23)

Scripture is clear that not everything supernatural comes from God. The bible warns that the false prophet who aids the Antichrist in his rise to power will be able to work great miracles to deceive the entire world. *The Word of God and the Spirit of God will never contradict each other.* That is critically important to keep in mind as we enter the closing days of this age.

Rejection of biblical authority and doctrine by false church leaders:

In the 1920's the fundamentalist versus modernist controversy was raging. Theologians following higher criticism abandoned the authority of scripture and the fundamentals of the faith. A series of articles defending the faith were written by scholars and published as a book series entitled *The Fundamentals.* Contributing authors included Dr. C.I. Scofield, Dr. R.A. Torrey, Dr. James Gray and others.

This battle for the Bible has continued into the 21st century with no sign of abating. Scripture clearly prophesied that many would depart from the faith in the last days.

Over sixty years ago, Dr. A.A. Davis wrote:

> The Bible itself is a revelation of divine truth. In some way or manner, we have grown into a generation of church people who abhor the word, "doctrine." The word "doctrine" simply means teaching. That is all it means. A true doctrine is a true teaching. A false doctrine is a false teaching. Where there is no doctrine there is no teaching.[9]

Depart from the faith and give heed to seducing spirits:

A recent survey indicated that many *evangelicals* believe there are other ways to heaven than through faith in Jesus Christ. Such are *evangelicals* in name only! Much of organized Christendom can be characterized as lukewarm and will be rejected by Christ at the rapture. It is this lukewarm *church* which will be left behind, join hands with the false prophet and submit to the Antichrist.

Pastor Robert Jeffress, senior pastor at First Baptist Church in Dallas, points out that Wheaton College[2] Professor Hawkins, who

---

[2] *A Christian college in Wheaton, Illinois*

was fired after stating that Muslims and Christians worship the same God, isn't alone in her unorthodox thinking. He says more than half (57 percent) of evangelicals today believe there is more than one way to God other than through Christianity.[10]

Following closely on the heels of this doctrinal apostasy is a departure from Biblical morality as the two are often related. When church leaders reject the authority of scripture, then immorality, homosexuality and all forms of sexual perversion are tolerated. It is no real surprise that apostate church leaders are defending the LGBTQ movement. When the Supreme Court makes it the law of the land we have forsaken our biblical heritage. America has had more biblical light than any nation in history. Dr. Jerry Falwell documented this as follows:

> America is a nation under God, built upon seven principles of the Judeo-Christian ethic. It is these seven principles that guided the thinking of our founding fathers as they penned the Declaration of Independence and the Constitution. All the compacts, agreements, and statutes on which our federal government and all 50 state governments are predicated are based on these principles.

Enumerated, these Old and New Testament biblical principles include:

1. The principle of the dignity of human life. (Ex. 20:13); (Matt. 5:21, 22)

> The Bible clearly points out, "Thou shalt not kill (commit murder)." In a land that has led the world in its position regarding the dignity and value of human life, we are today allowing the murder of millions of innocent babies. Our Supreme Court has ruled that innocent and defenseless unborn babies have no right to live. We are blatantly and shamelessly violating a moral principle on which this

23

nation was built, and we are suffering the consequences of this violation.

2. The principle of the traditional monogamous family. (Gen. 2:21-24; Eph. 5:22-33).

    A family begins when a man legally marries a woman. Diverse family forms such as common-law marriage or homosexual marriage are not acceptable. They are an abomination to God who divinely ordained order in the family relationship.

3. The principle of common decency. (Gen. 3:2l; Matt. 5:27-28; Eph. 5.3-5).

    Common decency in a race that is fallen because of sin begins with the covering of the human body. Today pornography is a four-billion-dollar business in our country. Lewd magazines portraying filthy acts are sold on newsstands at the eye level of a five-year-old child. Television programs and movies are filled with vulgarity, profanity, and obscenity.

4. The principle of the work ethic. (Gen. 3:19, Ex. 20:9,10; 2 Thess. 3:10).

    The Bible makes it clear that a man is to live by working with his hands. The result of the curse of sin upon man was that by the sweat of his brow he would earn his bread. There is a dignity in hard work, a dignity the welfare system has stripped from millions of Americans. The free enterprise system encourages ambition, incentive, competition, and hard work.

5. The principle of the Abrahamic covenant. (Gen. 12:1-3; Rom. 11:1, 2).

Several thousand years ago, God told Abraham that out of his seed would come a great nation, more numerous than the stars in the heaven and the sands of the seashore. God promised Abraham that through his seed all the families of the earth would he blessed. This is the Messianic promise. Jesus Christ provided the fulfilment for that blessing. Although all people are equally loved by God, Jews are God's chosen people. Palestine belongs to Israel. God deals with nations in relation to how those nations deal with Israel.

6. The principle of God-centered education. (Deut. 6.4-9; Eph. 6:4).

In recent years, the name of Almighty God has literally been removed from our public schools. Voluntary prayer has been banned. Creationism is no longer taught as a viable alternative to evolution which is now taught as a fact. As God was taken out of our schools, we saw moral permissiveness, academic deterioration, and the drug epidemic creep in.

In many cases, sex education classes in the public school are nothing more than academic pornography. Secular humanism, rather than God-centered education, has resulted in decadence and deterioration.

7. The principle of divinely ordained establishments.
   - The home (Gen. 2:21-24; Eph. 5:22-23).
   - State or civil government (Gen.10:32; Rom. 13:1-7).
   - Religious institution (Ex. 25:8, 9 [tabernacle, temple] Matt.16:17-19).

God divinely ordained the institutions of the home, the state (civil government), and the church. The home is the basic unit of a civilized society. A society is only as strong as the homes within that society."[11]

25

An ecumenical movement emerges uniting all religions into a false church:

Church history clearly documents centuries of division, hatred, persecution and bloodshed, all in the name of God. Catholics have killed Protestants, Protestants have killed Catholics, Christians have killed Muslims, Muslims have killed Christians, Hindus and Buddhists have been guilty of violence, all in the name of God. An unbelieving world watches in horror and disgust asking why don't they all get together and live in peace. Part of this history can be attributed to the fallen nature of man and his animosity toward his fellow man. But scripture reveals that the entire world lays in the lap of the wicked one, Satan, who works supernaturally to incite hatred, violence and killing. He inflames the hatred of man against man all in the name of "religion". Scripture reveals that Satan will inspire the man-made religions of the world to come together under the banner of the Antichrist and the False Prophet. That amalgamation of world religions will martyr Bible believers in the tribulation. Even now we clearly see a trend toward the merging of all religions:

Mohandas Gandhi on the Unity of All Religions

> Call Him Ishvara, Allah, God, and Ahura Mazda. His names are as innumerable as there are men. He is one without a second. He alone is great. There is none greater than He. He is timeless, formless, and stainless. Such is my Rama. He alone is my Lord and Master.
>
> To each man according to his faith is all that I can say. If all religions are one at source, we have to synthesize them. Today they are looked upon as separate and that is why we kill each other... This matter of Rama is one which transcends reason.

Indeed, religion should pervade every one of our actions. Here religion does not mean sectarianism. It means a belief in ordered moral government of the universe. It is not less real because it is unseen. This religion transcends Hinduism, Islam, and Christianity etc. It does not supersede them. It harmonizes them and gives them reality.[12]

Dr. David Reagan on Apostasy

How have we reached this crisis point in the Church? It is rooted in the German School of Higher Criticism which invaded this country big-time in the 1920's. According to the "scientific approach" of this school of skeptics, the Bible is not the revealed Word of God. Rather, it is Man's search for God, and therefore it is filled with myth, legend and superstition.

Today this viewpoint dominates the seminaries of America. The Bible is studied not to be believed and obeyed but to be analyzed, dissected, and criticized. The result is that the Scriptures have lost their authority.[13]

Pope Francis Urges All Religions to Unite

Pope Francis urged members of all religions and those belonging to no church to unite to defend justice, peace and the environment and not allow the value of a person to be reduced to "what he produces and what he consumes." Francis, elected a week ago as the first non-European pope in 1,300 years, met leaders of non-Catholic Christian religions such as Orthodox, Anglicans, Lutherans and Methodists, and others including Jews, Muslims, Buddhists and Hindus.[14]

Widespread unbelief in the Rapture and the Second Coming of Christ:

The closing days of the twentieth century and continuing into the twenty-first century saw an unparalleled interest in Bible prophecy and current events. This interest has not been limited to the church, but thinking people from all walks of life are asking about Armageddon, the Middle East and the Second Coming. Books on these topics are often best sellers. Yet, in the church there are some theologians who deny futurism, the rapture, the second coming and the millennium:

> The American obsession with the second coming of Jesus — especially with distorted interpretations of it — continues unabated. Seen from my side of the Atlantic, the phenomenal success of the *Left Behind* books appears puzzling, even bizarre. Few in the U.K. hold the belief on which the popular series of novels is based: that there will be a literal "rapture" in which believers will be snatched up to heaven, leaving empty cars crashing on freeways and kids coming home from school only to find that their parents have been taken to be with Jesus while they have been "left behind." This pseudo-theological version of *Home Alone*[3] has reportedly frightened many children into some kind of (distorted) faith."[15]

The truth is that one third of scripture is given to the subject of predictive prophecy. We are commanded in 2 Timothy 2:15 to study the scriptures in detail and learn to rightly divide them. There is no contradiction between God's command to evangelize the world and His command to study the prophecies of scripture. This is simply another indication of superficial evangelical thinking which minimizes all Bible doctrine, not just prophecy.

---

[3] A comedy movie in which an eight-year old is accidently left by his family

Summary of the Final Generation

Never in history has a pattern of events emerged which link the ancient prophecies of scripture with current news headlines like those of our day. Dr. David Reagan lists fifty reasons we are living in the last days. Those closely parallel and expand upon the ones already listed.

Fifty Reasons Why We Are Living in the End Times

1. Instability in nature (Matt. 24:7)
2. Increasing lawlessness and violence (Matt. 24: 12)
3. Increasing immorality (Matt. 24: 37)
4. Increasing materialism (2 Tim. 3:2)
5. Increasing hedonism (2 Tim. 3:4)
6. Depraved entertainment (2 Tim. 3:4)
7. Calling evil good and good evil (2 Tim. 3:3-4)
8. Increasing use of drugs (2 Tim. 3:3)
9. Increasing blasphemy (2 Tim. 3:2)
10. Increasing paganism (2 Tim. 3: 1-4)
11. Increasing despair (2 Tim. 3:1)
12. Signs of the heavens *[such as aircraft]* (Luke 21:11)
13. Increasing knowledge (Dan. 12:4)
14. Increasing travel (Dan. 12:4)
15. Increasing cults (Matt. 24:11)
16. Increasing apostasy or falling away in the church (2 Tim. 4:3-5)
17. Increasing hostility towards Jesus and Christians (Rom. 1:18-19)
18. Increasing hostility towards the Bible (Rom. 1: 18-19)
19. Increasing persecution towards Christians (Matt. 24:9)
20. Increasing interest in the occult (1 Tim. 1:4)
21. Increasing humanism (2 Tim. 3:2)
22. False Christs (Matt. 24:5)
23. Wars and rumors of wars (Matt. 24:6)
24. Weapons of mass destruction (Luke 21:26)
25. Increase in famine (Luke 21:11)
26. Increase in pestilence disease (Luke 21:11)
27. Computer technology (Rev. 13:7)
28. Television (Rev. 11:8-9)
29. Satellite technology (Rev. 11:8-9)
30. Virtual reality (Rev. 13: 14-15)
31. Unified Europe (Dan. 7: 2, 7)
32. Far Eastern military powers (Rev. 9:16; 16:12)
33. Movement to one-world government (Dan. 7:23-26)
34. Re-gathering of the Jews (Isa.11: 10-12)
35. Re-establishment of Israel (Isa. 66: 7-8)
36. Reclamation of the Lord in Israel (Ezek. 36:34-35)

37. Return of Jesus and Hebrew language (Zeph. 3:6)
38. Jerusalem reoccupied (Luke 21:24)
39. Israel as a military force (Zech. 12:3)
40. World politics focused on Israel (Zech. 12:3)
41. Russia a threat to Israel (Ezek. 38-39)
42. Another threat to Israel (Ezek. 25-36)
43. Denial of the Second Coming (2 Pet. 3: 3-4)
44. Denial of creation by God (Rom. 1:18-22)
45. Outpouring of the Holy Spirit (Joel 2: 28-29)
46. Bible translated in many languages (Matt. 24:14)
47. Gospel Worldwide (Matt. 24:14)
48. Rise of Messianic Judaism (Rom. 9:27)
49. Israel's Restoration (Amos 9:11)
50. Increase of understanding of Bible prophecy (Dan. 12:8-9)[16]

In addition to all these signs which have been listed, the nations of the world are merging into a very precise pattern outlined in the Holy Scriptures. Thinking, discerning people should be able to determine we are living in the last days. The claims of Jesus Christ should be seriously considered!

Chapter 3

Sign Two: Israel – The Super Sign of Prophecy

I srael's past, present and future is a major theme of scripture spanning from Genesis to Revelation. Jerusalem is mentioned over eight hundred times in scripture. Israel is mentioned 2,319 times in the King James Version of scripture. It was at the forefront of God's plan from Abraham to Christ.

> The story of Israel begins at the very beginning of the Bible, in the book of Genesis. The very proportion of the coverage tells us something about the importance of Israel. Only two chapters are given to the whole story of creation. One chapter in scripture records the fall of man. Eight chapters cover the thousands of years from creation to the time of Abram. Then we find that fully thirty-eight chapters deal with the life stories of Abraham, Isaac, and Jacob – the progenitors of the Jewish race. Apparently, God finds Abraham and his descendants to be of enormous importance[1]

With the rejection of The Lord Jesus Christ as Messiah; Israel was *temporarily* set aside in the plan of God. Jesus prophesied the destruction of Jerusalem which was fulfilled forty years later in A.D. 70 when Titus and the Roman legions invaded and destroyed Jerusalem. This began centuries of suffering upon the Jewish people; which continued throughout history. The trail of Jewish suffering was protracted and horrific:

- The destruction of Jerusalem in A.D. 70
- The temple was destroyed
- 30,000 slain by Romans in A.D. 50
- 40,000 more slain in A.D. 66
- 1,000,000 slain in A.D. 70
- 97,000 were taken captive at that same time
- 580,000 were slain in A.D. 130
- Canute banned all Jews from England in A.D. 1020

- Holy War began in A.D. 1096 (an attempt was made to murder all Jews who would not submit to baptism)
- Murderous riots led to robbery and murder of every household in London in A.D. 1189
- The Chief Rabbi of York and 500 followers were besieged at York Castle in A.D. 1190
- King Edward I drove 165,000 Jews from England in A.D. 1227. For nearly four hundred years not a Jewish foot trod English soil.
- 100,000 Jews were stripped of their possessions and cast out of France in A.D. 1306. After ten years they were permitted to return only to be slain by the thousands.
- Accused of being the source of the Black Death in Germany they suffered great tortures, cauldron and devouring flames. In the Strasburg community, two thousand in all, were put on scaffolds and burned. They were driven from the land and property valued at five million crowns was confiscated.
- In Spain, during the inquisition hundreds disappeared, put in prison, burned at stake, death in Iron Maiden. In 1492, Ferdinand and Isabella issued an edict of banishment against all Jews in Spain. Where to go they know not.
- Their endurance of it all lies in two facts:

  1. Their national law prevents disease, governs conduct

  2. Their national hope and faith in the coming of the Messiah[2]

Dr. Davis further comments on this trail of Jewish suffering:

It is estimated that as many as one million Jews died in the Great Revolt against Rome. When people today speak of the almost two-thousand-year span of Jewish homelessness and exile, they are dating it from the failure of the revolt and the destruction of the Temple. Indeed, the Great Revolt of 66-70 A.D., followed some sixty years later by the Bar Kokhba revolt, were the greatest calamities in Jewish history prior to the Holocaust. In addition to the more than one million Jews killed, these failed rebellions led to the total loss of Jewish political authority in Israel until 1948. This loss in itself exacerbated the magnitude of later Jewish catastrophes, since it precluded Israel from being used as a refuge for the large numbers of Jews fleeing persecutions elsewhere.[3]

In the prophetic plan of God unbelieving Israel will be brought to national repentance through the judgments of Daniel's seventieth week. A believing remnant will be converted to Christ and preserved through that seven-year period and meet the Messiah at His second coming to Earth.

We can outline God's prophetic dealings with Israel as follows.

- The call of Abraham
- The birth of Ishmael
- The birth of Isaac
- The birth of Jacob
- God's covenants with Abraham and his descendants
- The Covenant promises to Abraham, Isaac and Jacob
- Moses and the giving of the Law
- The establishment of the kingdom
- The promises to David
- The messages of the prophets
- The promise of the Messiah
- The inter-testament period
- The ministry of John the Baptist
- The ministry of Christ
- The rejection of Christ
- His death, burial and resurrection

- Pentecost and the Church
- The dispersion of Israel in 70 A.D.
- God visits the gentiles to call out the church
- A remnant of Israel becomes part of the church
- The epistles of the Apostle Paul
- The promise of the imminent return of Christ
- The history of the church: Israel in dispersion
- Signs of the times: Israel restored and current events since 1948
- The rapture occurs suddenly without warning
- Unbelieving Israel and the world are plunged into Daniel's seventieth week
- Israel will be brought to national repentance near the end of that week
- Messiah returns to save Israel and the world
- The covenanted kingdom is set up
- Promises to Abraham, Isaac, Jacob and David are then literally fulfilled

The prophets had foretold the restoration of Israel. That is the hub from which world events are understood in the plan of God. The Balfour Declaration was issued in 1917 by the British government, which laid the groundwork for the creation of the modern state of Israel. Israel officially declared statehood on May 14, 1948. The USA formally recognized it 11 minutes later and USA policy has dominated the Middle East ever since that time. The policies of every American president have affected Israel either positively or negatively:

Harry S. Truman

- First world leader to recognize the state of Israel
- This gave legitimacy to the newborn state
- Referred to it as "the proudest moment of his life"
- Most of his administration opposed it

- However, he instituted an arms embargo on Israel

Dwight D. Eisenhower

- Publicly supported the nation of Israel
- Applied pressure for Israel to withdraw from the Sinai
- First US president to threaten Israel when they hesitated from withdrawal
- He supported a UN resolution condemning them for not withdrawing
- He later expressed regret over having pressured Israel
- He continued the arms embargo instituted by Truman

John F. Kennedy

- Strong supporter of Israel in both word and deed
- He lifted the arms embargo of Truman and Eisenhower
- Extended the first informal security guarantees to Israel in 1962
- Beginning in 1963 he authorized the sale to Israel of advanced US weaponry
- He firmly opposed Israel's development of nuclear weapons
- His brother, Robert F. Kennedy, had pledged to maintain clear and compelling support for Israel
- His assassin, a Palestinian named Sirhan Sirhan said those words led him to kill Bobby

Lyndon B. Johnson

- Johnson was one of the greatest friends of Israel among modern day presidents
- He was often referred to as "America's first Jewish President"

- He worked to establish a refuge in Texas for European Jews fleeing Nazi Germany
- He was deeply influenced by a visit he made to the Dachau death camp in 1945
- Johnson strongly supported Israel during the 1967 Six-day War
- LBJ closely supervised the crafting of UN resolution 242 in 1967 calling for Israel to be guaranteed "secure and recognized boundaries"

Richard M. Nixon

- Nixon is considered today to have been anti-Semitic based on the infamous White House tapes
- He did recognize the importance of the only democratic state in the Middle East
- When Israel was attacked in the 1973 Yom Kippur War he responded with overwhelming aid
- He did that knowing it would alienate the Arab World and the Soviet Union
- Nixon is still admired by the Israelis "as the man who saved Israel"
- Golda Meir never forgot that Israel would have been destroyed if not for Nixon

Gerald R. Ford

- Ford took a hardline stance toward Israel demanding their withdrawal from Sinai which they had recovered during the Yom Kippur War
- Ford's letter to Yitzhak Rabin was harsh and threatening
- Many Senators called on Ford to make it clear that the USA stands firm with Israel
- When the Israelis stalled in response to his demands, he froze all scheduled delivery of arms

James Carter

- President Carter put the Sinai issue on the front burner when he came into office
- In 1979, he was able to broker a deal providing a complete withdrawal of Israel from the Sinai Peninsula
- In recent years Carter's writings show him to be a vehement anti-Semite who detests the Israelis
- When the 2014 war between Israel and Hamas broke out, Carter denounced Israel and called for the international recognition of Hamas

Ronald Reagan

- Ronald Reagan has the reputation of being the most pro-Israel president in American history
- Much of that reputation is based on glowing words that he often spoke in support of Israel
- Despite words like this Reagan had a number of run-ins with Israel
- In 1981, he significantly strengthened the Arabs by selling them some of our most sophisticated weapons
- He did that despite great opposition by both the Israelis and the Israeli lobby in Congress
- When Israel bombed the Iraqi nuclear reactor in 1981, Reagan supported the UN Security Council resolution that condemned Israel
- In 1985, Reagan began to provide Israel with $3 billion in foreign aid annually, all in the form of grants
- In 1988, Reagan authorized the State Department to enter dialogue with the PLO, reversing the U.S. policy of refusing to recognize terrorist organizations
- Reagan was infuriated when he was not informed in advance of the Israeli attack on the Iraqi nuclear reactor in

1981, and in that same year, chastised Israel for annexing The Golan Heights

- Menachem Begin accused Reagan of treating Israel like a "banana republic"

George H.W. Bush

- The Bush administration proved to be the decisive turning point in US-Israel relations
- His anti-Semitic Secretary of State, James Baker called for Israel to "abandon its expansionist policies
- Bush announced in 1991 that he considered East Jerusalem to be "occupied territory" despite the fact that Israel had officially annexed it in 1980
- Bush convened an international conference in Madrid, Spain and pursued an Arab-Israeli settlement
- That conference laid the groundwork for the Oslo accords in 1993 initiating the Land-for-Peace process
- Yasser Arafat was invited by James Baker to speak at the Baker Institute for Public Policy at Rice University

William J. Clinton

- Clinton positioned himself as a strong friend of the Jewish people and the nation of Israel
- He provided Israel with substantial financial aid
- He worked constantly behind the scenes to convince Israel to trade land-for-peace
- He presided over the signing of the Oslo accords at the White House in September of 1993
- In 1998, Clinton hosted the Wye River Conference between Arafat and Netanyahu which led to Israel agreeing to withdraw from Hebron
- In 2000, Clinton convened the Camp David Conference between Arafat and Ehud Barak

- Barak offered Arafat all he had ever demanded in diplomatic circles and Arafat walked out, immediately flew back to Israel and launched the Second Intifada
- On October 23, 1995 the US Congress passed the Jerusalem Embassy and Relocation Act
- Clinton refused to sign it and allowed it to become law without his signature

George W. Bush

- George W. Bush vowed not to follow his father's hardline policy toward Israel
- But hardly had he given this assurance, when in 2001, he turned around and called for the establishment of a Palestinian State
- He was the first USA president to do so publicly and formally, proceeding to make it an official part of U.S. foreign policy
- Bush gave new impetus to the Land for Peace strategy by demanding that Israel surrender the Gaza Strip

Barack Obama

- Obama emerged quickly as the most anti-Israel president in U.S. history
- His very first TV interview was granted to the Muslim network, Al Arabiya
- He followed by dashing off to Cairo, Egypt in June 2009 to give his famous apology speech to the Muslim nations of the Middle East
- In July 2009, he announced that the time had come for "daylight" between the United States and Israel
- In May of 2011, the president went on national TV to demand that Israel return to the suicidal borders that existed before the Six Day War in 1967

- In March of 2014, the spokesperson for the State Department announced that the Obama Administration no longer considered it necessary for the Palestinians to recognize the existence of the State of Israel
- Throughout his administration, Obama continued to condemn Israel's settlements as being "illegitimate"
- Obama continued to provide the Palestinian Authority with over $600M in aid each year
- In September of 2012, he proclaimed to the UN in a speech, "The future must not belong to those who slander the prophet of Islam"[4]

Donald J. Trump

- In May of 2017, he became the first President to visit the Western Wall while in office
- On June 6, 2017, the Senate passed a unanimous resolution commemorating the fiftieth anniversary of Israel's reoccupation and unification of Jerusalem in the Six Day War of 1967
- That resolution reaffirmed the Jerusalem Embassy Act of 1995, recognizing Jerusalem as the capital of the State of Israel, with the US Embassy located there
- President Trump made his proclamation to move the embassy on December 6, 2017
- Trump has assembled the most formidable Foreign Policy team in history
- Trump: Israel will pay a 'higher price' in peace talks after embassy move
- US, Israel officials downplay Trump's warning of 'price' over Jerusalem moves
- Trump endorses separate Palestinian state as goal of Mideast peace talks
- U.S. expects some Israeli criticism on coming Mideast plan

- Pence: Trump, greatest defender Israel ever had in WH!
- USA is entering an era of economic growth and prosperity greater than we have seen in decades.
- Election of Trump gives a window of opportunity to the church![5]

Daniel 9:25-27 has often been called the "John 3:16" of bible prophecy. It is this passage which is the key to understanding God's past, present and future dealings with the nation of Israel.

v. 25 – Know therefore and understand, *that* from the going forth of the commandment to restore and to build Jerusalem unto the Messiah the Prince *shall be* seven weeks, and threescore and two weeks: the street shall be built again, and the wall, even in troublous times.

v. 26 – And after threescore and two weeks shall Messiah be cut off, but not for himself: and the people of the prince that shall come shall destroy the city and the sanctuary; and the end thereof *shall be* with a flood, and unto the end of the war desolations are determined.

v. 27 – And he shall confirm the covenant with many for one week: and in the midst of the week he shall cause the sacrifice and the oblation to cease, and for the overspreading of abominations he shall make *it* desolate, even until the consummation, and that determined shall be poured upon the desolate.

This key passage details one of the most far reaching prophecies in scripture. No one has more clearly outlined that prophecy than Sir Robert Anderson, who wrote "The Coming Prince."

In his preface, Anderson outlined his thoughts, "Dismissing from our minds, therefore, all mere theories on this subject, we arrive at the following definitely ascertained facts":

1. The epoch of the Seventy Weeks was the issuing of a decree to restore and build Jerusalem. (Dan. 9:25)

2. There never was but one decree for the rebuilding of Jerusalem.

3. That decree was issued by Artaxerxes, King of Persia, in the month Nisan in the twentieth year of his reign.

4. The city was actually built in pursuance of that decree.

5. The Julian date of the first Nisan 445 was the fourteenth of March

6. Sixty-nine weeks of years – i.e. 173,880 days – reckoned from the fourteenth of March 445 B.C., and ended on the sixth of April A.D. 32

7. That day, on which the sixty-nine weeks ended, was the fateful day on which the Lord Jesus rode into Jerusalem in fulfillment of the prophecy of Zechariah 9:9; when, for the first and only occasion in all His earthly sojourn, He was acclaimed as "Messiah the Prince, the King, the Son of David."[6]

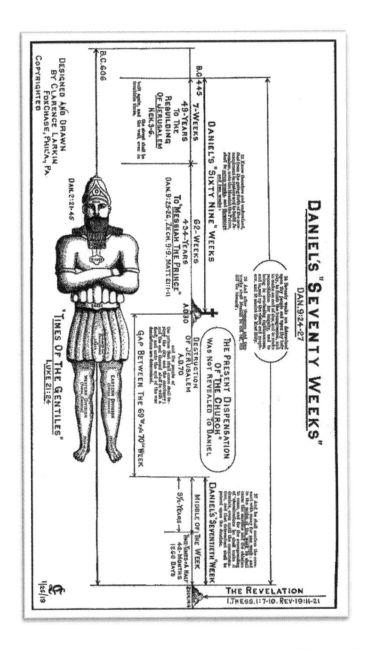

Chart: Clarence Larkin "Daniel's Seventy Weeks" - www.preservedwords.com/disptruth/title.htm *(public domain)*

45

Clarence Larkin's chart (above) illustrates the key points that Anderson documented which lead us to some basic conclusions:

Figuratively speaking, Artaxerxes' decree in 445 B.C. started the ticking of God's Jewish stopwatch. Christ made His triumphal entry 483 years (173,880 days) to the day from Artaxerxes' decree. God's Jewish stopwatch was paused. The entire seventy weeks were a total of 490 years. This leaves seven years yet to be fulfilled in God's dealings with Israel. (490 - 7 = 483). At this point, we must draw on the revelation given in other parts of the scripture and compare all of them. The writings of the Apostle Paul reveal that the church was a mystery not revealed to the Old Testament prophets. The book of Acts points out that God would visit the gentiles to call out a people for His name sake. Only after the completion of His plan and purpose for the church will God return to His specific dealings with national Israel. It is clearly seen in Revelation 6-19 that a seven-year period transpires called the Great Tribulation. That seven-year period perfectly fulfills the final segment of Daniel's Seventy Weeks. Dr. Billy Graham once made the comment that Daniel and Revelation should always be studied together. One must compare scripture with scripture to gain a broad overview of prophecy.

We might ask ourselves why the time gap between Daniel's sixty-ninth and seventieth week. The answer to that question reveals the unfolding of God's prophetic plan. Scripture and history record God's dealings with the Jews, His chosen people. The Apostle John wrote: "He came unto his own, and His own received Him not. But as many as received Him, to them gave He power to become the sons of God, *even* to them that believe on His name: Which were born, not of blood, nor of the will of the flesh, nor of the will of man, but of God." (John 1:11-13).

The Son of God made His appearance in human history. He was presented to the Jewish people as their Messiah at His triumphal entry. Daniel was clear that Messiah would be cut off.

Scholarship agrees that 109 prophecies were fulfilled at the first advent of Christ. Those prophecies document the birth, life, ministry, death, burial and resurrection of Christ with precision and accuracy.

Christendom is divided and confused over the interpretation of God's prophetic plan and purpose. There are Christians today who refuse to acknowledge any significance to the restoration of Israel and events in the Middle East. This division and confusion can be traced to the interpretive methods of theologians they follow.

Jesus wept over Jerusalem and prophesied that the Jews would be scattered among the nations. Israel's rejection of their Messiah was a major turning point in the plan of God. Titus and the Roman legions invaded and destroyed Jerusalem in A.D. 70.

Sir Isaac Newton understood the plan of God with uncanny prophetic insight. He wrote, "About the time of the end, a body of men will be raised up who will turn their attention to the Prophecies, and insist upon their literal interpretation, in the midst of much clamor and opposition."[7]

On the history of crucifixion, one source reports:

> In Britannica reports that the first historical record of Crucifixion was about 519 B.C., when Darius I, king of Persia, crucified 3,000 political opponents in Babylon.

Some further detail (from the same source) about the definition of cross is given in *Erdmann's Bible Dictionary*:

> Crucifixion is first attested among the Persians, perhaps derived from the Assyrian impalement. It was later employed by the Greeks, especially Alexander the Great, and by the Carthaginians, from whom the Romans adapted the practice as a punishment for slaves and non-citizens,

and occasionally for citizens guilty of treason. Although in the Old Testament the corpses of blasphemers or idolaters punished by stoning might be hanged "on a tree" as further humiliation (Deut. 21:23), actual crucifixion was not introduced in Palestine until Hellenistic times. The Seleucid Antiochus IV Epiphanes crucified those Jews who would not accept Hellenization.[8]

Gordon Robertson of CBN added this about the crucifixion:

> There is one piece of this prophecy in Psalm 22. Keep in mind, also, that David wrote this a thousand years before the death of Jesus, and crucifixion hadn't been even invented. So, there was nothing for David to have a reference for about hands and feet being pierced, or hanging on a cross until you're so dry that you are hungry and thirsty that you cry out, "My God. My God, why have You forsaken me?" There was no way for him to know that soldiers were going to gamble for your clothes. The prophecy is so specific, and it happened a thousand years before the crucifixion.[9]

Dr. Ron Rhodes added this about the Messianic prophecies:

> Of course, anyone can make predictions—that is easy. But having them fulfilled is another story altogether. The more statements you make about the future and the greater the detail, the better the chances that you will be proven wrong. But God was never wrong; all the messianic prophecies in the Old Testament were fulfilled specifically and precisely in the person of Jesus Christ.[10]

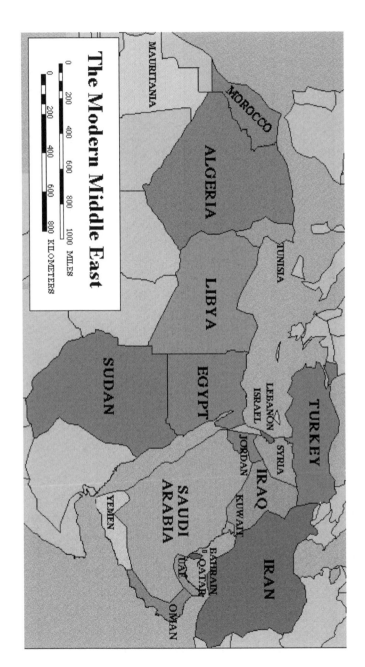

Map: The Modern Middle East. www.jewishvirtuallibrary.org

God's Past, Present and Future dealings with Israel

Israel is mentioned 2,319 times in the scriptures. The only way to harmonize scripture is to maintain Jew, Gentile and the Church in their proper context. Israel originated with the call of Abraham and human history cannot be intelligently comprehended without recognizing the history of Israel through the ages.

The issue of how Israel is viewed by Bible readers is ultimately one of hermeneutics or interpretation. Christ and the Apostles interpreted the scriptures literally. If we take the promises God made to Abraham, Isaac, Jacob and David and follow them to their literal and logical conclusion we must acknowledge a permanent place for Israel in the plan of God. There is significant controversy in the church over these issues. There are believers who spiritualize away all the promises in the Old Testament and see no significance to events in the Middle East and prophetic developments. Some of the fiercest theological conflicts are between Premillennial and Amillennial believers; who may share faith in the fundamentals, but interpret differently the significance of how and when the kingdom comes. That conflict would be more expected over issues such as the Virgin Birth or the Inerrancy of Scripture. Prophecy is not divisive, human nature is and that is nowhere seen more clearly than in the study and teaching of prophetic truth.

The issue of Israel's destiny is only understood through a panoramic view of scripture and history. To interpret scripture just as it reads and compare it to the restoration of Israel in 1948 is to see prophecy being fulfilled before our eyes. Israel is referred to as the super sign of Bible prophecy by some teachers.

Certain key events in the history of the restoration of Israel are as follows:

- 1917: The Balfour declaration makes provision for a Jewish Homeland
- 1945: The Holocaust under Nazi Germany creates an intense desire for their homeland
- 1948: Israeli statehood is declared
- 1948: USA President Harry Truman recognizes Israel eleven minutes later
- 1948: The Arabs attack the newborn state of Israel
- 1967: The Six Day War – Israel recovers Jerusalem
- 1980: Jerusalem became the undivided capital of Israel
- 1948-2016: Seventy years of wars and conflicts have continued
- An international crisis exists today with no permanent solution in sight

The stage is set for an international leader to come on the scene with an ingenious peace plan for Israel and the Middle East. It is not difficult for anyone to see that Israel faces insurmountable problems with her very existence. The various spheres of geopolitical power are being aligned into the pattern outlined by the prophets of scripture. If God were to sovereignly remove His church, the nations of the world are poised to fulfill their prophetic roles as foretold in the Word of God.

I had an experience years ago which relates to this. A brilliant co-worker of mine had been valedictorian of his college class. He had been an evangelical Christian and, at some point in his life, came under the influence of liberal theologians who espoused higher criticism. He eventually abandoned any faith in the deity of Christ or the authority of scripture. He and I had many cordial discussions about scripture and faith. I was burdened to bring him to faith.

One night I explained that Israel had been restored as a nation in 1948, and a precise pattern of events had come to pass with the nations surrounding Israel just as scripture had predicted 2,700 years ago. Events in the Middle East had continued to move that direction for over sixty years. Hundreds of events were predicted with perfect accuracy thousands of years in advance. Psychics and prognosticators are lucky if they get anything right. I then asked him, "How can you explain that if the Bible is not the Word of God?" He thought for a moment, and then cautiously replied, "I do not have an explanation for that!"

That experience strengthened my faith in the message of prophecy. I cannot make myself believe the restoration of Israel and the *convergence of events* surrounding it is "just an accident of history." I must conclude that an omniscient, sovereign God continues to orchestrate world affairs in fulfillment of His prophetic word.

On another occasion, I was taking a night class at a school in our area. We were given an assignment to prepare a brief presentation in which the teacher and classmates were to counter, disrupt and discredit our presentation in any way possible. Our instructor had the role of discrediting my presentation. As I presented the basic facts on prophecy and the Middle East, he sat there in amazement and silence. Afterward, he remarked that he could not discredit it because that is the way it is today. Balanced teaching of Bible prophecy is a powerful tool for ministry to skeptics!

Israel is referred to as the miracle of history by a number of writers. Ezekiel's Valley of Dry Bones is beginning to move into place just as the prophets foretold. It is unthinkable to me that the events of Daniel's Seventy Weeks could run their course without a prelude of current events which naturally lead up to it. Israel declared statehood in 1948 against all odds. The various spheres of geopolitical power described in scripture which surround and interact with her are moving into place as the prophets have foretold. Each are reviewed in following segments of this book

It is difficult to understand all the opposition to Israel even in the church world. Anti-Semitism is a special satanically inspired sin. There is no logical reason for the persecution and hatred of the Jewish people in the world. It is this ideology which will dominate the nations of the world at the end of the age. It will inflame and motivate all the armies of the world to march on Jerusalem at Armageddon.

Scripture clearly teaches that the rise and fall of empires is guided and directed by the hand of God. God allows or exercises control over everything that happens. He sets limits as to how far Satan and evil man can go. That isn't hard to see through the lens of bible prophecy. He works all things after the counsel of His will. Without faith in the providence of God one will never see or understand God's prophetic plan.

Israel, Jerusalem and the future of the Middle East remains in the forefront of world affairs today. Seventy years after the restoration of Israel, Jerusalem remains a burdensome stone and cup of trembling unto world leaders as prophesied in Zechariah 14:12.

Winston Churchill said, "It is manifestly right that the scattered Jews should have a national center and a national home and be reunited, and where else but in Palestine, with which for 3,000 years they have been intimately and profoundly associated?"[11]

Ronald Reagan has the reputation of being the most pro-Israel president in American history. Much of that reputation is based on glowing words that he often spoke in support of Israel. In September 1982, in a foreign policy speech about the Middle East he said:

> Israel exists and it has a right to exist in peace behind secure and defensible borders. And it has the right to demand of its neighbors that they recognize those facts. I have personally followed and supported Israel's heroic

struggle for survival ever since the founding of the state of Israel. In the pre-1967 borders, Israel was barely 10 miles wide at its narrowest point. The bulk of Israel's population lived within artillery range of hostile Arab armies. I am not about to ask Israel to live that way again."[12]

A good friend of mine, with insight into the hopelessness of the Middle East situation. observed that the USA would have to maintain a continual presence in that region. Prophecy indicates that the Middle East will eventually see all the armies of the world marching against the state of Israel. There is no permanent solution to the Middle East crisis apart from the return of Jesus Christ who is seated at the right hand of God the Father, although we must do what we can in whatever time remains. Come Lord Jesus!

Chapter 4

Sign Three: The Arab-Israeli Conflict

A View of Israel. Photo credit: Mark Walker

There is no question that the nation of Israel: past, present and future, plays a major role in Bible prophecy. It is equally true that prophecy teachers place a heavy emphasis on her role when expounding the prophecies of scripture. Many in Israel know and understand that evangelical Christians who take the prophecies of scripture literally, influencing them to support the nation of Israel are some of the best friends Israel has.

It is not difficult to understand why one man pointedly asked Dr. David Reagan, "Why do you Bible prophecy guys spend all your time talking about the Jews? There's a whole lot more Arabs than Jews. Don't you think God also cares about the Arabs?"

> It was a testy question during an open forum at one of my prophecy conferences. It was one I had heard many times before in various ways. In a recent letter, a person asked, "Don't the Palestinians have rights too? Does God love only the Jews?"

> There is no doubt that Bible prophecy teachers spend a lot of time speaking and writing about the Jewish people. It would be easy, therefore, to conclude that the Arab peoples are ignored in God's Prophetic Word. But, as we shall see, that is not the case. Bible prophecy focuses on the Jewish people because they are God's chosen people. In the process, it does not ignore the Arabs.

> A popular misconception is that Arab identity is determined by religion – that if you are a Muslim, then you are an Arab. That is not true. The most populous Muslim nation in the world is Indonesia, an island nation in Southeast Asia. Indonesians are not Arabs. They are Malays. Likewise, the nation of Iran is composed of Muslims, but they are not Arabs. They are Persians.

There are also Christian Arabs scattered throughout the Middle East. Until recent years, the city of Bethlehem was a Christian Arab town. Nazareth continues to this day to have a significant number of Christian Arabs.

Arab identity is not determined by religion. Most Arabs are Muslims, but not all; and all Muslims are certainly not Arabs. Arab identity is determined by ethnic heritage. And the amazing thing is that all Arabs – like all Jews – are descended from the family of Abraham! That means the Arab-Israeli conflict is a family dispute – the longest running and most intense family squabble in history. [1]

The history of the Arab-Israel conflict is easily traced to the tents of Abraham. Abraham and Sarah were two of the greatest people of faith in scripture. Each of them are mentioned along with the heroes of faith in Hebrews 11. God had promised them a child, which did not come immediately. They grew weary of waiting on God, and came up with a plan to "help God fulfill His word." They decided that Abraham would go in unto Hagar, Sarah's Egyptian handmaiden and produce a child. The child born of that union was Ishmael. The following scripture gives the Divine Viewpoint on this incident:

> And as for Ishmael, I have heard thee: Behold, I have blessed him, and will make him fruitful, and will multiply him exceedingly; twelve princes shall he beget, and I will make him a great nation.
>
> But my covenant will I establish with Isaac, which Sarah shall bear unto thee at this set time in the next year. (Gen.17:20-21, KJV)

Dr. David Reagan also references the very specific blessings to Ishmael's descendants:

Just as God made a covenant with Abraham's heirs through Isaac, He also made promises to Abraham's descendants through Ishmael, the father of the Arab nations (Gen.16:10-12; 17:20).

Here is a list, by Dr. Reagan, of the remarkable promises God made to the Arab peoples:

1)   The descendants of Ishmael will be multiplied "exceedingly" (Gen. 16:10;17:20).

2) They will become a great nation (Gen.17:20).

3) They will be given all the land east of Canaan (Gen. 16:12)

4) They will be given a personality like a "wild donkey," and because of this, "their hand will be against everyone (Gen. 16:12).

God has faithfully fulfilled all these promises:

- There are 200 million Arabs today
- They constitute a great nation composed of 21 states
- They occupy 5.3 million square miles of oil rich land
- They are characterized by an inability to get along with anyone, including themselves.

In contrast, there is only one Jewish state with a population of 6 million squeezed into an area of only 8,000 square miles. That's a population ratio of 33 to 1 and a land ratio of 662 to 1! And yet, the Arabs greedily demand the creation of another Arab state at the expense of the one Jewish state.[2]

As the data in the preceding note was documented from a 2002 article, it is important to note that "there are now an estimated 450 million Arabs, and 22 Arab states occupying 5,069,790 square miles of oil rich land."[3]

Israeli settlements are:

> Jewish-Israeli civilian communities built on lands occupied by Israel since the 1967 Six-Day War. Such settlements currently exist in the West Bank, East Jerusalem, and in the Golan Heights. Settlements previously existed in the Sinai Peninsula and Gaza Strip until Israel evacuated the Sinai settlements following the 1979 Israel-Egypt peace agreement and from the Gaza Strip in 2005 under Israel's unilateral disengagement plan.[4]

In light of the preceding documentation it becomes more difficult to understand the international criticism and condemnation of the modern state of Israel for building peaceful settlements in these areas!

Dr. David Reagan provides more background on the complex issues of the Arab-Israeli conflict:

The Palestinian Myth

- Regarding the Palestinians, during the nearly 1,900 years that the Jews were dispossessed of their land:
- There never was a Palestinian state
- Jerusalem was never the capital of any Arab state
- The Arabs who lived in the area considered themselves to be Syrians
- There was no Palestinian identity, culture, or language.
- The concept of a Palestinian claim on the land is a propaganda gimmick developed after the Six Day War in 1967 when Jordan lost the West Bank to Israel.

The Arab Claim on Jerusalem

The same is true of the Arab claim on Jerusalem. The Arabs contend that Jerusalem is the third most holy place behind Mecca and Medina. But again, all this emphasis on the significance of Jerusalem has developed in recent years.

There is no mention of Jerusalem in the Quran, whereas it is mentioned 667 times by name in the Hebrew Scriptures. Although the Arabs claim that Mohammed came to Jerusalem and from there ascended into heaven, there is no historical evidence whatsoever that Mohammed even came close to Jerusalem. The real geographical focus of Islam is the city of Mecca. Muslims pray toward this city, and it is to this city that they are required to make a pilgrimage once in their lifetime.

The real claim of the Arabs is based upon a portion of the Quran that states that once a land has been conquered for Allah, it must remain an Islamic land. The Arabs conquered the land and city in the middle Ages when they drove the Crusaders out. They now feel compelled by the Quran to reconquer it.

There are two other motivations for the Arab desire to retake both Israel and Jerusalem. The first is rooted in the fact that the re-establishment of the state of Israel is viewed by Muslim clerics as a judgment of God upon the Arab peoples for their lack of faithfulness to Islam. They must redeem themselves from this judgment by returning to the fundamentals of Islam and then, having been spiritually revived, Allah will empower them to regain both the land and the city.

The second factor is that the Arabs believe that their control of Jerusalem and its Temple Mount will certify their superiority over both Judaism and Christianity. The Temple Mount was the focal point of the Jewish faith for centuries because if was where the Temple was located. And it is believed that the Temple Mount is where the first Gospel sermon was preached by Peter on Pentecost, and thus was the sight of the birthplace of the church.[5]

With a vast amount of scripture, some 10,385 verses according to Dr. Jack Van Impe, given to predictive prophecy it is only fair to ask how that compares to the Quran. Prophecy is God's supernatural testimony of the authority of scripture written centuries in advance of its fulfillment. In this article on Islamic Eschatology, Dr. Reagan references *The Last Trumpet*:

> Strangely, the Quran contains very little prophecy about the end times. It mainly affirms that history will consummate with "the Hour" when the resurrection and judgment will take place. So, the Hadith is the major source of Islamic eschatology.

An Islamic Puzzle

> It is extremely difficult to piece together the Islamic concept of the end times. The information is greatly disjointed, being spread throughout the Hadith. Also, unlike Christian prophecy scholars, Islamic students of prophecy have not attempted to systematize their concepts into charts and diagrams which show how all the events are related to each other [...]

> The most helpful source I was able to discover was a book by Dr. Samuel Shahid called *The Last Trumpet*. He attempts to show that the major concepts of Islamic eschatology were borrowed from the Hebrew Scriptures, the Christian New Testament, and the concepts of Zoroastrianism. Dr. Shahid is the director of Islamic

studies at Southwestern Baptist Theological Seminary in Ft. Worth, Texas.

Dr. Shahid proves conclusively that Mohammed secured many of his ideas orally from Christians, Jews and followers of Zoroastrianism. In the process he got many of the stories and principles confused. For example, the Hadith states that the mother of Jesus was Mary, the sister of Moses!

Dr. Shahid also points out that the Hadith was compiled at a time when Islamic authorities knew much more about the Bible and Christian traditions and literature. Thus, many Hadith passages were manufactured and embellished and were heavily influenced by Christian sources.

Hadith passages concerning the end times are highly contradictory, and thus it is difficult to nail down a lot of specifics. Only a general outline of end time events can be compiled.[6]

In great contrast, the Holy Bible presents a detailed scenario of the end times in which the Arab nations play a huge role. Radical Islam is the catalyst which drives those nations.[7] Ezekiel 38-39 is the main scriptural passage outlining the alignment of the Arab world with Russia to invade Israel in the last days. Russia, believed by most commentators to be Gog, Magog, Meschech and Tubal, will play a central role in prophecy.

Israel is mentioned in Ezekiel 38 and 39 as center stage in the events that unfold at the end of the age. She is surrounded by hostile Islamic nations who are intent in "wiping Israel off the map." Ezekiel 38 lists the players as Gog, Magog, Meschech, and Tubal, a great company, Persia, Ethiopia, Libya, Gomer, Togarmah and all his bands, all thy bands and many with thee.

Research has been done on these passages and the consensus of competent scholars usually agrees with little variation.

In his article, "The Battle of Gog and Magog," Dr. Mark Hitchcock reviews the countries involved in Ezekiel 38 as follows:

Persia

The words *Persia, Persian, or Persians* are found 35 times in the Old Testament. The ancient land of Persia became the modern nation of Iran in March 1935, and then the name was changed to the Islamic Republic of Iran in 1979. Iran's present population is 68 million.

Ethiopia (Cush)

The Hebrew word *Cush* in Ezek. 38:5 is often translated *Ethiopia* in modern versions. According to *The New Brown-Driver-Briggs-Gesenius Hebrew-English Lexicon*, ancient Cush was the "land and people of southern Nile-valley, or Upper Egypt, extending from Syene indefinitely to the south." Ancient Cush was called *Kusu* by the Assyrians and Babylonians, *Kos* or *Kas* by the Egyptians, and *Nubia* by the Greeks. Secular history locates Cush directly south of ancient Egypt extending down past the modern city of Khartoum, which is the capital of modern Sudan. Thus, modern Sudan inhabits the ancient land of Cush. Sudan is a hardline Islamic nation that supported Iraq in the Gulf War and harbored Osama bin Laden from 1991 to 1996.

Put

It is clear from ancient sources that *Put* or *Phut* was a North African nation (Jer. 46:9; Ezek. 27:10; 30:5; Nah 3:9).

From the *Babylon Chronicle* it appears that *Putu* was the "distant" land to the west of Egypt, which would be modern day Libya.

The Septuagint renders the word *Put* as *Libues*. *The Brown-Driver-Briggs Lexicon* also identifies Put with Libya. Modern Libya, which is an Islamic nation, has been under the rule of Colonel Muammar al-Gadhafi since 1969 [until his assassination in 2011].

Gomer

Gomer has often been identified as Germany or more particularly East Germany before the fall of communism. Gomer is probably a reference to the ancient Cimmerians or *Kimmerioi*. Ancient history identifies biblical Gomer with the Akkadian *Gi-mir-ra-a* and the Armenian *Gamir*. *The Cambridge Ancient History* states that the Assyrian *Gimirai* is the Hebrew Gomer. Beginning in the eighth century B.C., the Cimmerians occupied territory in Anatolia, which is modern Turkey. Josephus noted that the Gomerites were identified with the Galatians who inhabited what today is central Turkey.

Beth-Togarmah

The Hebrew word "beth" means "house," so Beth-Togarmah means the "house of Togarmah." Beth-Togarmah is mentioned in Ezekiel 27:14 as a nation that traded horses and mules with ancient Tyre. Ezekiel 38:6 states that Beth-Togarmah comes from "the remote parts of the north with all its troops." Ancient Togarmah was also known as Til-garamu (Assyrian) or Tegarma (Hittite) and its territory is in modern Turkey, which is north of Israel.

Charting the Nations in Ezekiel 38 and 39

With these identifications in mind, all the nations that will participate in the battle of Gog and Magog can be seen in the following:

Ancient Name / Modern Nation

Rosh (Rashu, Rasapu, Ros, and Rus) / Russia

Magog (Scythians) /Central Asia and possibly Afghanistan

Meshech (Muschki and Musku) / Turkey

Tubal (Tubalu) / Turkey

Persia / Iran

Ethiopia (Cush) / Sudan

Libya (Put or Phut) / Libya

Gomer (Cimmerians) / Turkey

Beth-Togarmah (Til-garimmu or Tegarma) / Turkey

Based on these identifications, Ezekiel 38 and 39 predicts an invasion of the land of Israel in the last days by a vast confederation of nations from north of the Black and Caspian Seas, extending down to modern Iran in the east, as far as modern Libya to the west, and down to Sudan in the south. Therefore, Russia will have at least five key allies: Turkey, Iran, Libya, Sudan, and the nations of Central Asia. *Amazingly, all of these nations are Muslim nations* and Iran, Libya, and Sudan are three of Israel's most ardent opponents. Iran is one of the "axis of evil" nations that are trying desperately to attain nuclear weapons. Many of these nations are hotbeds of militant Islam and are either forming or strengthening their ties as these words are being written. This list of nations reads like the Who's Who of this week's newspaper. *It does not require a very active imagination to envision these nations conspiring together to invade Israel in the near future.*[8]

A hostile Arab Coalition will arise to oppose Israel in the End Times

As the scriptural and historical information is compared it is easy to see a role for the Arab nations is prophesied in scripture, although Islam is not specifically referenced. Islam has come to the forefront of world affairs at the beginning of the 21st century with no end in sight.

Virtually all of the nations listed in Ezekiel 38 as allied with Russia are Islamic. The Arab-Israeli conflict has continued for nearly seventy years and humanly speaking, there does not appear to be a solution. World leaders are perplexed in trying to finding a working solution to the Middle East crisis.

Just as the prophets predicted, Jerusalem has become a burdensome stone and cup of trembling to world leaders. Israel will not give up Jerusalem as their eternal capital. Islam lays claim to Jerusalem as its third holiest site. Each of these claims is deeply rooted in the hearts of these people.

The Arab-Israeli conflict has the potential to bring the entire world to nuclear war. It is this nightmare scenario which appears to be outlined in the scriptures and current events are certainly shaping up for a final showdown in the Middle East.

Chapter 5

Sign Four: Russia, Gog, Magog and the Middle East

R ussia is the great power to the North of Israel. Due north from Jerusalem intersects with Moscow. A brief summary of Russian history is helpful in understanding her role in the prophetic scriptures.

- 1917: Bolshevik Revolution
- 1924: Lenin Dies
- 1929: Stalin becomes USSR leader
- 1945: Berlin falls to Russia
- 1953: Stalin dies and is succeeded by Nikita Krushev
- 1964: Krushev replaced by Leonid Brezhnev
- 1985: Mikhail Gobachev becomes leader of USSR
- 1990: Boris Yeltsen is elected President
- 1991: USSR is dismantled and Russia becomes an independent federation
- 1999: Yeltsen resigns and Vladimir Putin becomes his successor
- 2008: Medvedev assumes leadership in Russia
- 2012: Putin has regained power in Russia and is active in world affairs in 2018

The years between WWII and the breakup of the USSR were known as the Cold War. As nuclear powers, the United States and the USSR both carried the threat of mutually assured destruction (M.A.D.) hung over the world.

> The Cold War was a state of political and military tension after World War II between powers in the Western Bloc (the United States, its NATO allies and others) and powers in the Eastern Bloc (the Soviet Union and its satellite states). Historians do not fully agree on the dates, but a common timeframe is the period between 1947, the year the Truman Doctrine (a U.S. policy pledging to aid nations threatened by Soviet expansionism) was announced, and 1991, the year the Soviet Union collapsed.[1]

Bible prophecy describes the role of Russia in detail. Dr. C.I. Scofield proved to be a man ahead of his time when he published the notes in his reference Bible. He foresaw Russia invading Israel in Ezekiel 38 and 39 in 1909 before the Bolshevik revolution (1917) and before the restoration of Israel (1948). He simply based his conclusions on the writings of scripture.

Prophetic scholars are agreed for the most part on the role of this northern confederacy and its Arab allies.

Dr. Mark Hitchcock provides substantial documentation for Russia in prophecy. His conclusions are similar with those of other premillennial scholars, and are as follows:

> "This was the final message in this series of six-night oracles delivered by Ezekiel," notes Ralph Alexander. "A central concern throughout all these night messages had been the possession of the land of Israel." This series of night oracles was given to encourage the exiles that ultimately God would remove these invaders and restore this land to Israel. A wonderful message indeed to which those who love Israel still look forward to today!
>
> This prophecy is divided into two major sections. In the first section Ezekiel reveals the invasion by Gog with his allies (38:1-16). The second section reveals to us God's judgment that will befall Gog and his associates (38:17-39; 16). This great prophecy begins with Ezekiel noting that it was not his idea to deal with the matter of Gog's invasion of Israel instead it was God who imitated and communicated this prophecy through verbal revelation, "the word of the Lord came to me saying."

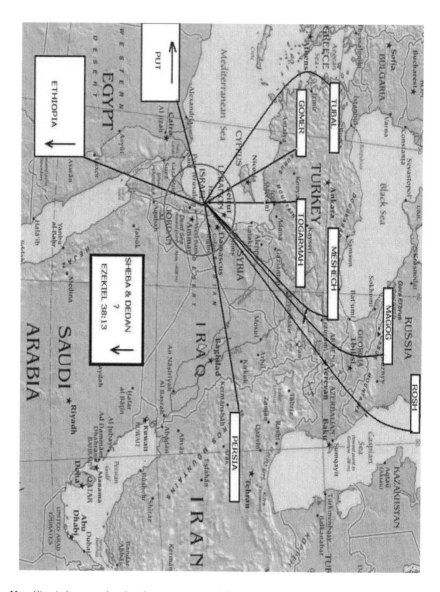

Map: Historical names and modern-day counterparts. marklhitchcock.com

Son of Man

Ezekiel is called "son of man" throughout the book. "Son of man" is used 93 times in Ezekiel to refer to the prophet, with the first use found in 2:1. Why is Ezekiel so often addressed by God as "son of man" when he is about to receive revelation from the Lord? It appears that "son of man" underscores his humanity in relation to God. In other words, God is the One who is the Revealer while Ezekiel, as a human, is the recipient of the Divine message that he is to pass on to other human beings. Thus, Ezekiel is passing on to us the infallible prophecy of these two chapters, which will surly come to pass.

Set Your Face toward Gog

Ezekiel is told to set his face "toward" or "against" Gog. *The Brown, Driver, and Briggs (BDB) Hebrew Lexicon* says, the Hebrew word translated "toward" is a preposition that denotes "motion to or direction towards (whether physical or mental)." *BDB* also tells us that when "the motion or direction implied appears from the context to be of a hostile character," then it has a negative connotation and would be translated "against." Ezekiel is told to turn his face in the direction of the nation Gog because the Lord is against him. Later in the sentence, the text tells Ezekiel to "prophesy against him," meaning Gog. The sense of this passage is that God is initiating the attack by Gog against Israel and the Lord is against or opposed to Gog and his allies. But just who is Gog? The identification of Gog has been a greatly debated issue.

The Hebrew proper noun "Gog" occurs twelve times in the Hebrew Old Testament. All but one use occurs in Ezekiel 38 and 39. In Ezekiel 38, Gog is found in verses 2, 3, 14, 16, and 18. In Ezekiel 39, Gog is found twice in verse 1 and three times in verse 11, and verse 15. The only non-Ezekiel occurrence is in 1 Chronicles 5:4 and says, "The sons of Joel were Shemaiah his son, Gog his son, Shimei his son." Other than demonstrating it was a real, proper name, the 1 Chronicles reference contributes nothing to our study of its use in Ezekiel and is not related to the Gog of Ezekiel's prophecy. Whoever he is, Gog appears in the context of Ezekiel to be a person, leader and ruler that God has told Ezekiel to prophesy against. Because of the frequent use of "Gog" in this passage, "we conclude, therefore, that Gog is the most important person or nation in this coalition," declares Mark Hitchcock.

The passage says that Gog is from the land of Magog. Some have said that Gog is a reference to the Antichrist. Charles Feinberg is right when he says, "but for this, there is not a shred of biblical or nonbiblical evidence."

Some have suggested that Gog is a name "arbitrarily derived from the name of the country, Magog, but this is not valid because Gog appears in 1 Chronicles 5:4." The name Gog means "high, supreme, a height, or a high mountain." The only references to the Gog of Ezekiel's prophecy appear in the passage itself and there is virtually no information about Gog outside the Bible in history. However, when Gog leads his invasion of Israel he is said to come "from the remote parts of the north" (Ezek. 38:6). Louis Bauman tells us that L. Sale-Harrison says in his booklet, *The Coming Great Northern Confederacy*: "It is interesting to note that the very word 'Caucasus' means 'Gog's Fort.' The words "Gog' and 'Chasan' (Fort) are two Oriental words from which it is derived.'" So there does appear to be a faint reference to Gog in the general area of Russia that Gog is likely to be from.

Who then is Gog? Bauman answers, "Without doubt, Russia will furnish the man-*not the Antichrist*-who will head up that which is known to most Bible students as 'the great northeastern confederacy' of nations and lead it to its doom upon the hills of Israel's land." Hitchcock believes "the reason Gog is singled out eleven times by God in these two chapters is because God is the general over this coalition of nations in its great military campaign against Israel." Hal Lindsey explains, "Gog is the symbolic name of the nation's leader and Magog is his land. He is also the prince of the ancient people who were called Rosh, Meshech, and Tubal." Arnold Fruchtenbaum informs us: "Who Gog will be can only be determined at the time of the invasion, for 'Gog' is not a proper name but a title for the ruler of Magog, just as the terms *pharaoh, kaiser,* and *czar* were titles for rulers and not proper names."

The Land of Magog

Gog, the leader of the invasion of the land of Israel, is said to be "of the land of Magog." The proper noun Magog is used four times in the Hebrew text of the Old Testament. Magog is used twice in the passage we are investigating (Ezek. 38:2 – 39:6) and twice in genealogies (Gen. 10:2; 1 Chron. 1:5). Genesis 10:2 says, "The sons of Japheth were Gomer and Magog and Madai and Javan and Tubal and Meshech and Tiras." 1 Chronicles 1:5 is basically a repeat of the genealogical information from Genesis 10:2. The fact that Magog is used in the table of nations (Genesis 10) provides a basis for tracing the movement of one of the earliest post-flood descendants of Noah.

It appears that Ezekiel is using the names of peoples, primarily from the table of nations, and where they lived at the time of the giving of this prophecy in the sixth century B.C. Therefore, if we are able to find out where these people and places were in the sixth century B.C., then we will be able to trace who would be their modern antecedents today. I believe we will be able to accomplish this task and be able to know who will be involved in this battle if it were to come to pass in our own day.

It is probably fair to say that most scholars and experts would trace Magog's descendants to the ancient people that we know as the Scythians. Chuck Missler notes that a wide collection of ancient historians "identified Magog with the Scythians and southern Russia in the seventh century B.C." These ancients include: Hesiod, Josephus, Philo, and Herodotus. Josephus lived in the first century and said, "Magog founded the Magogians, thus named after him but who by the Greeks are called Scythians." Bauman tells us that Magog and his descendants must have immigrated north after the Flood and that "the Magogites were divided into two distinct races, one Japhetic, or European, and the other Turanian, or Asiatic."

Who are the Scythians? Edwin Yamauchi tells us that the Scythians were divided into two groups, a narrow and broad grouping. "In the narrow sense, the Scythians were the tribes who lived in the area which Herodotus designated as Scythia (i.e., the territory north of the Black Sea)," notes Yamauchi. "In the broad sense the word Scythian can designate some of the many other tribes in the vast steppes of Russia, stretching from the Ukraine in the west to the region of Siberia in the east."

We have seen that Magog is a reference to the ancient Scythians, who gave rise to later descendants that settled along the eastern and northern areas of the Black Sea. "The descendants of ancient Magog-the Scythians-were the original inhabitants of the plateau of central Asia, and later some of these people moved into the area north of the Black Sea. The homeland of ancient Scythians is inhabited today by the former Soviet republics of Kazakhstan, Kirghizia, Uzbekistan, Turkmenistan, Tajikistan, and the Ukraine." But who is *the prince of Rosh*?

The Attack on Rosh

The identification of Rosh is one of the most controversial and debated issues in the entire Gog and Magog prophecy, even though it should not be. I believe when one looks at the evidence it is overwhelming that this is a reference to the modern Russians. However, we need to first look at the evidence for such a conclusion.

Preterist prophecy critic, Gary DeMar contends, "In Ezekiel 38:2 and 39:1, the Hebrew word *rosh* is translated as if it were the name of a nation. That nation is thought to be modern Russia because *rosh* sounds like Russia." He then quotes Edwin M. Yamauchi, noted Christian historian and archeologist, that rosh "can have nothing to do with modern 'Russia.'" In an October 2002 radio broadcast, known as *The Bible Answer Man*, host Hank Hanegraaff, asked Gary DeMar what he thought about Tim LaHaye identifying Rosh as Russia, since the two words sound so much alike. DeMar responded, "The idea that you can take a word in Hebrew that sounds like the word in English, and then go with that and to create an entire eschatological position based upon that is – it's nonsense."

As I will discuss later, identification of the Hebrew word *rosh* with Russia is not based upon similarity of sound. That is a flimsy straw man that DeMar constructs so that he can appear to provide a credible criticism of our view on this matter. DeMar then declares: "The best translation of Ezekiel 38:2 is 'the chief (head) prince of Meshech and Tubal."

Concerning the possibility of a Russian/Islamic invasion of Israel in the end times, Marvin Pate and Daniel Hays say categorically, "The biblical term *rosh* has nothing to do with Russia." And later they state dogmatically, "These positions are not biblical [...] a Russian-led Muslim invasion of Israel is not about to take place."

A central issue in whether *rosh* refers to Russia is whether *rosh* is to be understood as a proper noun (the Russia view) or should it be taken as an adjective (the non-Russia view) and be translated in English as 'chief.' This is a watershed issue for anyone who wants to properly understand this passage."

Reasons Rosh Refers to Russia

Now, I want to deal with reasons why *rosh* should be taken as a noun instead of an adjective and then I will deal with whether it refers to Russia. The word *rosh* in Hebrew simply means *head, top,* or *chief._* It is a very common word and is used in all Semitic languages. It occurs approximately seven hundred and fifty times in the Old Testament, along with its roots and derivatives.

The problem is that the word *rosh* in Ezekiel can be translated as either a proper noun or an adjective. Many translations take *rosh* as an adjective and translate it as the word *chief.* The King James Version, The Revised Standard Version, and the New International Version all adopt this translation. However, the New King James, the Jerusalem Bible, New English Bible, American Standard Version, and New American Standard Bible all translate *rosh* as a proper name indicating a geographical location. The weight of the evidence favors taking *rosh* as a proper name. There are five arguments that favor this view.

First, the eminent Hebrew scholars C. F. Keil and Wilhelm Gesenius both hold that the better translation of Rosh in Ezekiel 38:2-3 and 39:1 is as a proper noun referring to a specific geographical location._ Gesenius, who died in 1842, is considered by modern Hebrew scholars as one of the greatest scholars of the Hebrew language, unquestionably believed that Rosh in Ezekiel was a proper noun identifying Russia. He says that *rosh* in Ezekiel 38:2,3; 39:1 is a "pronoun of a northern nation, mentioned with Meshech and Tubal; undoubtedly the *Russians*, who are mentioned by the Byzantine writers of the tenth century, under the name *the Ros*, dwelling to the north of Taurus [...] as dwelling on the river Rha (*Wolga*)."

This identification by Gesenius cannot be passed off lightly, as DeMar attempts to do. Gesenius, as far as we know, was not even a premillennialist. He had no eschatological, end time axe to grind. Yet, objectively, he says without hesitation that Rosh in Ezekiel 38-39 is Russia. In his original Latin version of the lexicon, Gesenius has nearly one page of notes dealing with the word Rosh and the Rosh people mentioned in Ezekiel 38-39. This page of notes does not appear in any of the English translations of Gesenius' Lexicon. Those who disagree with Gesenius have failed to refute his sizable body of convincing evidence identifying Rosh with Russia._ I do not know what DeMar would say about this evidence since he never addresses it.

Second, the *Septuagint*, which is the Greek translation of the Old Testament, translates *Rosh* as the proper name *Ros*. This is especially significant since the *Septuagint* was translated only three centuries after Ezekiel was written (obviously much closer to the original than any modern translation)._ The mistranslation of Rosh in many modern translations as an adjective can be traced to the Latin Vulgate of Jerome, which did not appear until around A.D. 400. James Price, who has a Ph.D. in Hebrew from Dropsie, which is the leading Jewish academic university in America says, "The origin of the translation 'chief prince of Meshech and Tubal' is traced to the Latin Vulgate. The early translators of the English Bible were quite dependent on the Latin Version for help in translating difficult passages. They evidently followed Jerome in Ezekiel 38:2, 3; 39:1."

Price further explains the reason for the erroneous translation as follows: Evidently by the second century, the knowledge of the ancient land of Rosh had diminished. And because the Hebrew word *rosh* was in such common use as "head" or "chief," Aquila was influenced to interpret *rosh* as an adjective, contrary to the LXX [Septuagint] and normal grammatical conventions. Jerome followed the precedent set by Aquila, and so diminished the knowledge of ancient Rosh even further by removing the name from the Latin Bible.

By the sixteenth century, ancient Rosh was completely unknown in the West, so the early English translators of the Bible were influenced by the Latin Vulgate to violate normal Hebrew grammar in their translation of Ezekiel 38 and 39. Once the precedent was set in English, it was perpetuated in all subsequent English versions until this century when some modern versions have taken exception. This ancient, erroneous precedent should not be perpetuated.

Clyde Billington explains why Jerome went against most of the evidence and went with a deviant translation: Jerome himself admits that he did not base his decision on grammatical considerations! Jerome seems to have realized that Hebrew grammar supported the translation of "prince of Rosh, Meshech, and Tubal" and that it did not support his own translation of "chief prince of Moshoch and Thubal." However, Jerome rejected translating Rosh as a proper noun because, "we could not find the name of this race [i.e. the Rosh people] mentioned either in Genesis or any other place in the Scriptures, or in Josephus." It was this non-grammatical argument that convinced Jerome to adopt Aquila's rendering of Rosh as an adjective *chief* in Ezekiel 38 and 39.

Third, many Bible dictionaries and encyclopedias in their articles on Rosh, support taking it as a proper name in Ezekiel 38. Some examples: *New Bible Dictionary*, *Wycliffe Bible Dictionary*, and *International Standard Bible Encyclopedia*.

Fourth, Rosh is mentioned the first time in Ezekiel 38:2 and then repeated in Ezekiel 38:3 and 39:1. If Rosh were simply a title, it would probably drop in these two places because in Hebrew, when titles are repeated, they are generally abbreviated.

Fifth, the most impressive evidence in favor of taking Rosh as a proper name is simply that this translation is the most accurate. G. A. Cooke, a Hebrew scholar, translates Ezekiel 38:2, "the chief of

Rosh, Meshech and Tubal." He calls this "the most natural way of rendering the Hebrew." Why is it the most natural way of rendering the Hebrew? Rosh appears in construct form in the Hebrew with Meshech and Tubal meaning that the grammar forms a list of three nouns. Some want to say that *rosh* is a noun functioning as an adjective since there should be an "and" if it were intended to be a list of three nouns. The same exact Hebrew construction appears in Ezekiel 38:5, as well as Ezekiel 27:13, and these are clearly recognized as a list of three nouns by grammarians even though "and" does not appear in either list. Normal Hebrew and Arabic grammar support *rosh* as a noun (see also Ezek. 38:3 and 39:1). Actually, Hebrew grammar demands that *rosh* be taken as a noun. No example of Hebrew grammar has ever been cited that would support taking *rosh* as an adjective. Instead, in Hebrew grammar, one cannot break up the construct chain of the three nouns that have this kind of grammatical arrangement. Hebrew scholar Randall Price says, "On linguistic and historical grounds, the case for taking *Rosh* as a proper noun rather than a noun-adjective is substantial and persuasive."

In light of such overwhelming evidence, it is not surprising that Hebrew scholar James Price concludes the following: It has been demonstrated that Rosh was a well-known place in antiquity as evidenced by numerous and varied references in the ancient literature. It has also been demonstrated that an adjective intervening between a construct noun and its *nomen rectum* is highly improbable, there being no unambiguous example of such in the Hebrew Bible. Furthermore, it has been demonstrated that regarding *Rosh* as a name is in harmony with normal Hebrew grammar and syntax. It is concluded that *Rosh* cannot be an adjective in Ezekiel 38-39, but must be a name. Therefore, the only appropriate translation of the phrase in Ezekiel 38:2-3, and 39:1 is "prince of Rosh, Meshech, and Tubal."

Clyde Billington says, "the features of Hebrew grammar [...] dictate that Rosh be translated as a proper noun and not as an adjective. [...] It should, however, be noted that the grammatical arguments for the translation of Rosh as a proper noun in Ezekiel 38-39 are conclusive and not really open for serious debate. What would Gary DeMar say about such evidence? I do not know, since I have never seen him address these arguments. DeMar is merely prone to making dogmatic statements to the contrary based upon no real evidence for his position.

Therefore, having established that Rosh should be taken as a proper name of a geographical area, the next task is to determine what geographical location is in view.

Historical and Geographical Support for Rosh as Russia

Clyde Billington has written a series of three scholarly articles in a theological journal presenting extensive historical, geographical and toponymical evidence for why Rosh should be and is traced to the Russian people of today.

He interacts with the leading commentaries and authorities of the day in his research and presentation. Billington notes, "it is also clear that Jerome, in deciding to translate Rosh as an adjective rather than a proper noun, based his decision on a nongrammatical argument, i.e. that a people called the Rosh are not mentioned either in the Bible or by Josephus." However, there is considerable historical evidence that a place known as Rosh was very familiar in the ancient world. While the word appears in a multitude of various languages, which have a variety of forms and spellings, it is clear that the same people are in view.

It is very likely that the name Rosh is actually derived from the name Tiras in Genesis 10:2 in the Table of Nations. Billington notes the Akkadian tendency to drop or to change an initial *t* sound in a name especially if the initial *t* was followed by an *r* sound. If you drop the *T* from Tiras, you are left with *ras*. It makes sense for Ras or Rosh to be listed in Genesis 10, since all the other nations in

Ezekiel 38:1-6 are also listed there. This means Jerome's claim that Rosh did not appear in the Bible or in Josephus is erroneous. Since Tiras and his descendants apparently are the same as the later Rosh people, then Rosh does appear in both the Table of Nations and Josephus.

Rosh (Rash) is identified as a place that existed as early as 2600 B.C. in Egyptian inscriptions. There is a later Egyptian inscription from about 1500 B.C. that refers to a land called Reshu that was located to the north of Egypt. The place name Rosh (or its equivalent in the respective languages) is found at least twenty times in other ancient documents. It is found three times in the Septuagint (LXX), ten times in Sargon's inscriptions, once in Assurbanipal's cylinder, once in Sennacherib's annals, and five times in Ugaritic tablets._ Billington traces the Rosh people from the earliest times in recorded history up to the days of Ezekiel, as they appear multiple times throughout this historical period."

Clearly, Rosh or Tiras was a well-known place in Ezekiel's day. In the sixth century B.C., the time Ezekiel wrote his prophecy, several bands of the Rosh people lived in an area to the north of the Black Sea. As we approach the eighth century, Billington cites a number of historical references showing that "there is solid evidence linking one group of Rosh People to the Caucasus Mountains." From the same general period of time, Billington notes, "There is even one cuneiform document from the reign of the Assyrian King Sargon II (ruled 722-705 B.C.) which actually names all three peoples [Rosh, Meshech, Tubal] mentioned by Ezekiel 38-39."

Billington concludes this section of his historical studies as follows:

> Therefore, there is irrefutable historical evidence for the existence of a people named Rosh/Rashu in 9th-7th century B.C. Assyrian sources. These same Assyrian sources also mention Meshech and Tubal, whose names appear in

conjunction with the name Rosh in Ezekiel 38-39. Clearly, the Assyrians knew of the Rosh people, and so also did the prophet Ezekiel. It should be noted that Ezekiel wrote the Book of Ezekiel only about one hundred years later than extant Assyrian texts which mention the Rosh, Meshech, and Tubal peoples.

Does the Name Russia Come from Rosh?

The ancient Rosh people, who have been traced back to Tiras, a son of Japheth (Gen. 10:2), who migrated to the Caucasus Mountains in Southern Russia, are one of the genetic sources of the modern Russians of today. However, does the name for Russia come from the Biblical word Rosh as used in Ezekiel 38:2? We have seen that Marvin Pate and Daniel Hays have said categorically, "The biblical term *rosh* has nothing to do with Russia." Their statement is typical of the sentiment of many critics today. But is such a conclusion where the evidence leads? I do not think so! Here's why.

First, we need to know that the Hebrew Old Testament was translated sometime in the third century B.C. and it is known as the Septuagint (LXX is the abbreviation). The Septuagint translates the Hebrew word Rosh in all its uses by the Greek word *Ros* or *Rhos*. The early church, more often than not, used the Septuagint as their primary Old Testament. It is still used in the Greek speaking world today as their translation of the Old Testament. Billington tells us:

> "Early" Greek Orthodox writers, using the LXX's spelling [Ros] of the name Rosh, identified the Rosh people of Ezekiel 38 and 39 with the northern Rus people of Russia and the Ukraine." These people would be ones that lived near, but north of the Greek speaking peoples. Such close proximity would mean that they would have been clear in whom they were identifying and they identified them with the Rosh people. Maranatha![2]

As we have seen previously, the Greek translation of the Old Testament Hebrew took *Rosh* as a proper noun and identified them with the people of Southern Russian and the Ukraine. Such a translation indicates that the Greek-speaking Jews in North Africa believed that *Rosh* was a proper noun and referred to a known people.

After providing an impressive amount of data to support the notion that the Rosh people refer to modern day Russians, Clyde Billington declares:

> Therefore, it is almost certain that the ancient people whom the Greeks called Tauroi/Tursenoi were identical to the people known as Tiras in the Bible. These same Tiras people of Genesis 10:2 were also called in other languages by a variety of names based upon the name Tiras. For example, note the names: Taruisha [Hittite], Turus/Teresh [Egyptian], Tauroi/Tursenoi [Greek], and Tauri/Etruscan [Latin].

Second, Billington tells us,

> From a variety of sources, it is known that a people named the Ros or Rus lived in the same area near the Black Sea where the Tauroi people lived.

Billington also tells us:

> Early Byzantine Christian writers identified the Rosh people of Ezekiel 38-39 with an early group of people of southern Russia whom they called the 'Ros.' We further learn that the Byzantine Greeks used the LXX spelling [Ros] of the name because they unquestionably identified the Ros/Rus/Russian people of southern Russia with the Rosh people mentioned in Ezekiel 38-39.

Thirdly, "it is well-known that the first Russian state was founded by a people known as the Varangian Rus." Many current scholars like Edwin Yamauchi support the notion that the name Rus, from which the modern name for Russia is derived, is a Finnish word and refers to Swedish invaders from the North, not from the Rosh people in the South. He says that the name Rus did not come to the region until the Middle Ages when it was brought by the Vikings. However, while Yamauchi is a respected scholar, his dogmatic conclusion stands in direct opposition to the substantial historical evidence presented by the Hebrew scholars Gesenius, James Price, and Clyde Billington.

Billington provides six objections to Yamauchi's claim of a Northern origin of *Rus* instead of a Southern one. First, the Byzantine use of the word *Rus* for those who became the Russians pre-dates the Northern claim by hundreds of years. Second, Byzantine sources never speak of these people as having immigrated from the North to the South. They "were long time inhabitants of the Black Sea-Russia-Ukraine-Crimea area, and none of the Byzantine sources states that the original homeland of the Ros was Scandinavia." Third, since various forms of the "Rosh people are found in use all the way back to the second century B.C., it is most unlikely that the Finns invented the name Rus. Fourth, "there is no logical reason why the Ros people should have adopted the foreign Finnish name of 'Ruotsi' after migrating to southern Russia." Fifth, "all modern scholars agree that the Varangians never called themselves (and they were never called by others) 'Ros' while they still lived in Scandinavia near the Finns." Finally, Byzantine and Western records indicate that there were people in Southern Russia who were already calling themselves by the name of "Rus" many years before the Northern invasion.

It is clear, when one sifts through the evidence that the Varangians who migrated from Scandinavia into Southern Russia were called by the name of *Rus* when they moved into that area, which had already been known by that name for many years. Billington summarizes:

> As was argued above, the Varangian Rus took their name from the native people named the Ros who had from ancient times lived in the area to the north of the Black Sea. In other words, there were two Ros peoples: the original Sarmatian Ros people and the Varangian Rus people.

It should be clear by now that *Rosh* does indeed refer to the modern-day Russian people. Both grammatical and historical evidence have been provided. This is why I agree with the overall conclusions of Billington, who says:

> 1. Ezekiel 38-39 does mention a people called the "Rosh" who will be allies of Meshech, Tubal, and Gog in the Last Days.

> 2. There were Rosh peoples who lived to the north of Israel in the Caucasus Mountains and to the north of the Black and Caspian Seas.

> 3. Some of the Rosh people who lived to the north of Israel came in time to be called "Russians."

> 4. The name Russian is derived from the name Ros/Rosh, which is found in Ezekiel 38-39.

> 5. And, in conclusion, it is clear that Russian peoples will be involved along with Meshech, Tubal, and Gog in an invasion of Israel in the Last Days.

Who Is Meshech?

I now move on to the much easier task of identifying to whom Meshech refers. Meshech appears ten times in the Hebrew Old

Testament, including its first usage in the Table of Nations (Gen. 10:2). In Genesis 10, Meshech is listed as a son of Japheth. The genealogical descent from Genesis 10 is repeated twice in 1 Chronicles 1:5, 17. Other than references in Psalm 120:5 and Isaiah 66:19, the other occurrences of Meshech are all found in Ezekiel 27:13; 32:26; 38:2-3; 39:1. The three references in Ezekiel 38 and 39 all group "Rosh, Meshech and Tubal" together, as does Isaiah 66:19 but in a different order.

Mark Hitchcock tells us: "All we know about Meshech from the Old Testament is that Meshech and his partners Javan and Tubal traded with the ancient city of Tyre, exporting slaves and vessels of bronze in exchange for Tyre's merchandise." That's all the Bible tells us about ancient Meshech. However, ancient history has a great deal to say about the location and people of ancient Meshech.

Some Bible teachers in the past have taught that Meshech is a reference to Moscow and thus refers to Russia. This is the view of *The Scofield Reference Bible* by Harry Rimmer and Hal Lindsey. Rimmer says of Meshech, "his descendants came to be called 'Mosche,' from which derived the old term 'Muscovites.' While this later word is and has been applied to all Russians who come from Moscow and its vicinity." The identification of Meshech with Moscow is merely based upon a similarity of sound. There is not real historical basis to support such a view, therefore, it must be rejected.

Allen Ross, based upon historical and biblical information in his dissertation on the table of nations says, Tubal and Mesek are always found together in the Bible. They represent the northern military states that were exporting slaves and copper seen in Ezekiel 27:13; 32:26; 38:2; 39:1 and Isaiah 66:19. Herodotus placed their dwelling on the north shore of the Black Sea (III, 94). Josephus identified them as the Cappadocians. Mesek must be located in the Moschian Mountains near Armenia. Their movement was from eastern Asia Minor north to the Black Sea.

The area southeast of the Black Sea is modern day Turkey. "At every point in the history of Meshech," notes Hitchcock, "they occupied territory that is presently in the modern nation of Turkey." Such a conclusion is not a controversial one, since virtually all scholars agree with this view.

Who Is Tubal?

"Tubal" appears eight times in the Hebrew Bible in Genesis 10:2; 1 Chronicles 1:5; Isaiah 66:19; Ezekiel 27:13; 32:26; 38:2-3; 39:1). Tubal is identified as the fifth son of Japheth and the brother of Meshech in the table of nations in Genesis 10:2. As noted above by Ross, Tubal is always grouped together with Meshech in the Bible and Ezekiel 38 is no exception.

Some prophecy teachers have taught that Tubal is the derivative that became the modern Russian city, Tobolsk. This view was popularized by *The Scofield Reference Bible* and a number of other teachers. However, as was the case with Meshech, such a view is developed from similarity of the sound of Tubal and Tobolsk. This view lacks a solid historical basis. The historical record, as was the case with Meshech, is that Tubal and his descendants immigrated to the area southeast of the Black Sea in what is modern day Turkey. Meshech and Tubal clearly provide the population base for the country we now call Turkey.

Today, Turkey is considered a secular country. However, Turkey has a long history as a Muslim-dominated country that for hundreds of years headed up the Muslim empire. Turkey is just a step away from returning to its Islamic political heritage, which would provide a basis for aliening with the other Muslim-dominated territories that will one day invade Israel. Maranatha!

The writings of Dr. Hitchcock provided much documentation as evidence that Russia as the main player in the Ezekiel 38 and 39 campaign. Current events are setting the stage for the scenario described there, especially as Putin remains on the world stage.

Summary of Russia in World Affairs Today

At the breakup of the USSR, critics of the premillennial view of this passage hastily rushed to dismiss the serious scholarship of Scofield, Lindsey and many others. It is now clear that Russia has not ceased to be a major player on the global stage. It is equally true that Vladimir Putin remains as a dominant figure in Russia and tensions between Russia and the USA are significant at this time following the 2016 USA elections.

Russia's Involvement with Israel

Substantial documentation supports the Russian-Islamic invasion of Israel as listed in Ezekiel 38 and 39. Keep in mind that Israel is the epicenter into which all end-time prophecies converge. We have a glimpse of the direction world affairs are moving when the church of Jesus Christ is raptured and mankind is plunged into the Seventieth Week of Daniel.

Russia, one of the main players in the end times, is prominent today as are all the signs which are converging. This does not mean that every single current event must be viewed as a fulfillment of prophecy. What this does mean is that a pattern of events has come into play, which is setting the stage for the events of the tribulation period. Once the church is removed, those events will continue without interruption. Not everyone in the world will hear the warnings, but prophecy has been used to bring many to faith in Christ.

Prophecy is clear that the great power from the north, in concert with many Muslim nations in the Middle East will invade Israel in the last days. That conflict will work out in a series of battles which will ultimately lead to all the armies of the world marching toward Israel. It is not difficult to envision that scenario in light of current events which have continued into the 21st century.

Chapter 6

Sign Five: Antichrist, EU and the New World Order

Bible prophecy students have long watched for the "Revived Roman Empire." It is generally believed that the center of power for the Antichrist would arise in the territory of what was the old Roman Empire.

It is interesting that the Belgium Netherlands, and Luxembourg agreement which started the reunification of Europe was ratified in 1948, the same year Israel was restored as a nation; as well as many other prophetic events. The joining of Belgium, Netherlands and Luxembourg (Be-Ne-Lux) was the beginning of that union.

- 1948: Be-Ne-Lux agreement
- 1950: Schuman Declaration
- 1957: Treaty of Rome
- 1973: Britain, Denmark and Ireland join
- 1980: Ten Nations
- 1981: Greece joins EC
- 1986: European identity expressed for first time
- 1986: Portugal and Spain join
- 1990: East and West Germany united. East Germany becomes part of EC
- 1993: Maastricht treaty turns the communities into a union
- 1995: Austria, Finland and Sweden join the EU
- 1999: Euro adopted as a single currency
- 2002: National currencies are replaced by euro notes and coins
- 2004: Ten new member states join the EU: Czech Republic, Cyprus, Estonia, Hungary, Latvia, Lithuania, Malta, Poland, Slovakia, and Slovenia
- 2007: TEC (Transatlantic Economic Council) is created
- 2007: Bulgaria and Romania join the EU
- 2009: Herman von Rompuy becomes the first president of the EU council
- 2013: Croatia becomes the 28th country to join the EU
- 2014: European parliament elects President of the European Commission

From its simple beginnings in 1948 to the twenty-eight-nation unity we see today, it is apparent that an economic and military super state is arising. Dr. Thomas Ice summarizes this as follows:

> We see in our own day the increasing isolation of Israel within the world leading to an effort for her to look for security from man-made covenants instead of looking to the Lord for stability. One day a European leader will step forth and appear to solve the Middle East crisis through a covenant. In the meantime, God is preparing through contemporary events in our own day a Revived Roman Empire that will be the final phase of the kingdom of man that will put forth its greatest effort against Almighty God. There are specific indications of active stage-setting all around us, if we know where and how to look. These developments are paving the way, for the great events that will unfold during the tribulation. While God is preparing our world for judgment, the Believer should continue to be about the Lord's business while we watch and wait for the any-moment return of the Lord in the clouds to snatch away His bride. Maranatha![1]

In his article, "Brexit and the European Union" he incudes a passage from Daniel 7:7-8:

> After this I kept looking in the night visions, and behold, a fourth beast, dreadful and terrifying and extremely strong; and it had large iron teeth. It devoured and crushed, and trampled down the remainder with its feet; and it was different from all the beasts that were before it, and it had ten horns. While I was contemplating the horns, behold, another horn, a little one, came up among them, and three of the first horns were pulled out by the roots before it; and behold, this horn possessed eyes like the eyes of a man, and a mouth uttering great boasts (Daniel 7:7–8).

Then summarizes: Since you all have heard the news that Great Britain has voted 52 to 48% to leave the European

Union (EU), you may be wondering how this fits into Bible Prophecy. Since I have never believed the European Union is any kind of actual fulfillment of prophecy, instead, it is most likely some kind of forerunner that could easily prepare the way for the actual Revived Roman Empire in the form of a ten-nation confederacy as predicted in the Bible (Dan. 2:42–43; 7:24–25; Rev. 13:1–10). Pundits are all over the board when it comes to analyzing what this development means for Britain, the EU, and the world at large. Some are predicting the collapse of the EU, while others think the EU will double down on their tyranny and do away with national borders all together.

Disproving Bible Prophecy?

Every time something like this has taken place in my lifetime, those who teach the literal understanding of Bible prophecy are said to have been proven wrong by the events of contemporary history. I recall, when the Soviet Union collapsed in 1991, it was said by the critics of Bible prophecy that it would now be impossible for the Russian-led invasion of Israel to take place (Ezek. 38 and 39). Of course, such is not the case since prophecy teachers had taught that it was Russia and not the Soviet Union that was to lead the invasion.

I have read some who are saying similar things today about the exit of Britain from the EU. They are implying that Brexit will bring about an end of the EU and thus disprove our view of Bible prophecy. Actually, the Brexit vote does not affect a thing in regards to an eventual Revived Roman Empire and its ten-nation union. I would never say that current stage-setting is the actual fulfillment of biblical prophecy that is clearly set within the context of the seventieth week of Daniel, or the seven-year tribulation. I have always taught that the rapture must take place before the tribulation period will commence, and so it must. Thus, whatever happens before that time in relation to the EU is simply further preparation for the eventual fulfillment of God's plan during the still future tribulation.

I read an article that came out shortly after the Brexit vote arguing that this would not destroy the EU, instead, they argue, it will strengthen the resolve of the EU. Frankly, it could go either way, as far as I am concerned, and it would not impact the future fulfillment of God's prophetic plan since He is not fulfilling those prophecies today, but He is preparing the stage for when they will be fulfilled. In an article entitled: "European Superstate to be Unveiled: EU Nations to be Morphed into One Post-Brexit," it says, the German and French are proposing a blueprint to make the EU into a single super state. The foreign ministers of France and Germany are due to reveal a blueprint to effectively do away with individual member states in what is being described as an ultimatum. The article continues to explain: Under the radical proposals EU countries will lose the right to have their own army, criminal law, taxation system or central bank, with all those powers being transferred to Brussels. Apparently, the leadership in the EU believes that a crisis is a terrible thing to waste. Conventional thinking, which is usually wrong, sees the Brexit vote as the beginning of the unraveling of the EU; but on the other hand, some within the leadership of the EU, see it as an opportunity to double-down and create a stronger union, a completely tyrannical union that will merge much of Europe into a single entity.

In another development related to the Brexit vote and the rise of Islamic terrorism, the EU foreign policy chief Federica Mogherini said, "As Europeans we must take greater responsibility for our security."

Mogherini continues with the following rationale:

> While NATO exists to defend its members—most of which are European—from external attack, Europeans must be better equipped, trained and organized to contribute decisively to such collective efforts, as well as to act

autonomously if and when necessary. A more credible European defense is essential also for the sake of a healthy transatlantic partnership with the United States.

I certainly do not know which direction the EU will take in the next few months, whether they will fall apart and dissolve or band together into an even stronger union. However, I do know that one day in the future there will be a Revived Roman Empire that will come together, after the rapture, to form Satan's final thrust to overthrow God. God is currently in control of all these developments as He has been since the beginning of creation. His plan will come to pass perhaps in a way that none of us will be able to figure out ahead of time. But it will come to pass in His time!

The Biblical Forecast

One of the core elements of end-time prophecy relating to the tribulation is the biblical prediction that there would be a revived form of the fourth of the four Gentile kingdoms as predicted in Daniel 2 and 7. Since Rome was clearly the fourth kingdom, it follows that some form of her kingdom will be revived. What all the king's horses and all the king's men could not do, God will allow the antichrist to accomplish for a brief period of time (in the future).

Daniel 7 and Revelation 13 and 17 notes that a ten-nation confederacy will be revived during the tribulation period. This alliance will facilitate the world domination of the Antichrist for a few years. Dr. John Walvoord explains:

> The prediction that there will be a ten-kingdom stage of the revival of the Roman Empire is one of the important descriptive prophecies of the end time. This prophecy anticipates that there will be ten countries originally related to the Roman Empire that will constitute the Roman Empire in it revived form. [...] The prediction requires a political union and then a dictator over the ten countries.

94

Developments in our own day relating to the renunciation of Europe through the EU are an indication that God is preparing the world for just such a configuration as predicted thousands of years ago in the Bible. After the rapture of the church, the ten-nation confederacy will arise and then the Beast or the Little Horn, also known as the Antichrist, will arise among them (Dan. 7:8, 20, 24–25). The political union is in the process of being developed in our day via the EU. It is not there yet, since the rapture has not taken place, but current developments are giving rise to forcing various people groups into a common union that they do not like. Yet, Scripture says it will occur any way with the use of force, as noted by the description of iron mixed with clay:

> And in that you saw the feet and toes, partly of potter's clay and partly of iron, it will be a divided kingdom; but it will have in it the toughness of iron, inasmuch as you saw the iron mixed with common clay. And *as* the toes of the feet *were* partly of iron and partly of pottery, *so* some of the kingdom will be strong and part of it will be brittle. And in that you saw the iron mixed with common clay, they will combine with one another in the seed of men; but they will not adhere to one another, even as iron does not combine with pottery (Dan. 2:41–43).

Conclusion

As we keep in mind that Israel is back in their land and a nation, just as Bible prophecy depicts during the tribulation. The EU appears to be some kind of forerunner to the reviving of the Roman Empire that simply went out of existence hundreds of years ago. For the first time since the Tower of Babel, the world's mindset, especially among the intellectual elite, is wholly given over to some form of global governance since World War II. Russia is poised to provide her leadership for the impending invasion of

Israel as predicted in the Gog and Magog war of Ezekiel 38 and 39. Persia, which is modern Iran, is also positioning itself for this attack on Israel, along with the other nations mentioned in Scripture.

In concert with Daniel, John tells us in Revelation, and the ten horns which you saw are ten kings, who have not yet received a kingdom, but they receive authority as kings with the beast for one hour (Rev. 17:12). Earlier, John saw a beast coming up out of the sea, having ten horns and seven heads, and on his horns were ten diadems, and the heads were blasphemous names (Rev. 13:1). This is descriptive of Antichrist and his kingdom during the tribulation. The ten horns represent ten powers or kingdoms. The ten diadems on the heads represent ten kings over each kingdom. And the blasphemous names tell us that each is in league with Antichrist in his opposition to God during this time. Therefore, we should not be surprised that there are rumblings related to the preparation of the formation of a future ten-nation confederacy. Maranatha![2]

The European Union in Prophecy

Out of the territory which contained the old Roman Empire a power block will arise from which the Antichrist will emerge. He will come on the scene after the rapture and broker a temporary peace in the Middle East. He will make a seven-year covenant with Israel and it will appear that the Middle East crisis has been solved. Our world is weary with war and fighting. Hal Lindsey was leading a tour in Israel years ago. A young rabbi told him, "Sir, we are so tired of war I think we would follow the Devil himself if he could bring peace!" Hal said his blood ran cold, and he replied, "Sir, that is just exactly what you will do!"

A number of prophecy scholars conclude that America may join with Europe, but in a diminished capacity. It is the leader of the west who will make the treaty with Israel which defines the direction of prophecy for the last seven years of history.

The various spheres of geopolitical power will be contending for dominance in the Middle East and it appears the EU will play a central role.

A global pattern of events is emerging in world affairs today. The rise of the EU is only part of that scenario, although it is a major part. Once an overview of that scenario is seen and understood it is difficult to deny the literal nature of Bible prophecy in my opinion.

Chapter 7

Sign Six: China, the Kings of the East and Armageddon

Revelation 16:16 mentions an economic and military power known as "The Kings of the East". The consensus of many premillennial scholars is that this is China and her allies. Dr. Tim LaHaye added this summary:

> The rise of China to become a dominant world political force during the past decade has enormous significance from a prophetic point of view. Many students of prophecy believe it signifies a trend that world geopolitical conditions are shaping up for the world's last great conflict described over nineteen hundred years ago by the Apostle John when he wrote: "Then the sixth angel poured out his bowl on the great river Euphrates and its water was dried up, so that the way of the kings from the East might be prepared." (Rev. 16:12)

> These "kings from the east" have befuddled Bible prophecy scholars for many years, for few mentioned anything about them. That is, until the communist take-over of China during World War II. Since then, it has become apparent that this largest of all countries in the world has a prophetic role, however minor it may be, in end time events. We can readily understand that, for China has been content to stay within its vast borders for thousands of years and live pretty much to itself. Their communist dictators have changed all that for they seem to have the same obsession that characterized communists before them - world conquest.[1]

The historical events in China in this generation set the stage for her role in prophecy:

- 1949: Mao Zedong, head of the Communist Party, establishes the People's Republic of China. Rivals belonging to the Nationalist Party move to Taiwan, off China's eastern coast.
- 1958-1961: Mao's plan to change China's economy and farming system fails. Millions of people die of starvation.

- 1972: Richard M. Nixon becomes the first U.S. President to visit Communist China.
- 1989: About 1 million students hold pro-democracy protests in Beijing's Tiananmen Square. The uprising is crushed by the army
- 1964-1996: 45 nuclear tests conducted
- 1997: China regains control of Hong Kong, which had been under British rule for 99 years.
- 2005: Russia, China held first joint military exercises
- 2010: China officially surpasses Japan to become the world's second largest economy.

The significance of the rise of China at this strategic time in history to the point that she is becoming a principle player among the nations of the world was not lost on the perceptive prophecy expert Dr. John Walvoord. He saw the prophetic significance of their rise to prominence back in 1967 when he wrote:

> The fact that the rise of Asia has occurred in our twentieth century with so many rapid and unexpected developments is evidence that the world is moving toward its final climax and the end of the times of the Gentiles. In Asia, as in other parts of the world, the stage is being set for the final drama in which the kings of the east will have their important part.

> If he were writing on that subject today, he might be inclined to say the curtain is about to rise. We are convinced that the rise of China to world prominence economically and militarily in our day is prophetically speaking a most significant event. For we are the first generation that has witnessed the sleeping giant of China reach the potential of fulfilling this prophecy. No one doubts that unless something drastic and unforeseen occurs soon, China will gain control of most of the countries of the east, with which she shares many religious and cultural

similarities. That she could be led in these very days by her master, the dragon, "that old serpent, the devil" the deceiver of men, to so rebel against God that she would actually join the armies of the world in opposition to the Coming of Jesus Christ is realistic. What is needed to bring them to that capability? Very little, just the deceiving spirits mentioned by John the Revelator. They are almost there today and could gain control of the entire Orient in ten or at most twenty years.

And remember, this does not take place until seven years after the rise of the antichrist, which follows the rapture of the church. More than enough time to prepare to fulfill 16:12! Just one more reason we have to believe Christ may return for His church in our generation.

China has climbed into a country with a growing influence capable of becoming a superpower rivaling the United States. From an article on monitoring strategic trends in China:

In recent years, China has bought, borrowed, or stolen technology, which has catapulted its military capabilities into the modern high-tech arena. No one can match China for sheer numbers of people, and now it can challenge most of the world in technological achievements. The Clinton administration blindly sold sensitive technology to China and reportedly received campaign financing in return.

The human rights abuses have received less attention lately as various foreign leaders flock to pay state visits to the country and give little or no condemnation of China's human rights record. It seems that it is more important to placate than to demand reform. In the meanwhile, forced abortions and sterilization continue to be state policy, and political and religious persecution continues unchecked.

The "red dragon" no longer sleeps. It is already anticipating a war with the United States in the next decade or so and may one day prove to be a mighty adversary for anyone who gets in the way.

Just as China has emerged as a mass manufacturer, India is emerging as a giant in services. Technical and managerial strengths in both China and India are becoming more important that cheap assembly labor. And, their relative strengths are complementary, not competitive. For example, China has excelled in mass manufacturing, with multi-billion-dollar electronics and heavy industrial plants; India has specialized in software, design, services, and precision industry. Their efficiency in back-office processing alone is legendary and outsourcing such work is expected to quadruple by 2010 to over $56 *billion* per year!

These two emerging giants will transform the entire global economy. China and India account for one-third of the world's population. For the past two decades, China has been growing at 9.5% per year, and India at 6% per year. Both are projected to continue at an annual rate of 7-8% for at least the next ten years. By mid-century, China should overtake the U.S. as #1. Together, China and India could account for almost half of the total global output.

India's younger workforce will give it a chance to catch up to China. Due to its one-child policy, Chinas working age population will peak at 1 billion in 2015 and then shrink steadily. India has nearly 500 million people (twice the population of the U.S.) under the age of 19 *and* higher fertility rates. By mid-century, India is expected to have 1.6 billion people, 220 million *more* workers than China."[2]

China in Prophecy

Israel is the epicenter from which all prophecy is interpreted. The Kings of the East will make their way into the Middle East near the end of the tribulation period. China and her allies are commonly believed by most prophecy scholars to be the final great block of geopolitical power to invade the Middle East. Current events are setting the stage for that final conflagration which will ultimately involve all the armies of the world.

Chapter 8

Sign Seven: The USA, Jerusalem and the Middle East

President Harry Truman became the first world leader to acknowledge the newborn state of Israel in 1948. A seventy-year state of conflict and tension has existed ever since that time. Humanly speaking, there does not appear to be a permanent solution to the problem. World leaders are perplexed with the Middle East crisis. The prophet Zechariah wrote that Jerusalem would become a burdensome stone and cup of trembling to the nations.

No nation in history has played any larger role in shaping the world scene today than the USA. While many prophecy scholars see no discernable role for the USA in prophecy, we may draw some conclusions of how America may fit into the overall prophetic scenario in scripture. The most common suggestions by prophecy scholars for the destiny of the USA are as follows:

- The USA is not specifically mentioned in prophecy
- To continue as a major player in world evangelism and teaching ministry to the nations
- To continue in peace, prosperity and blessing as the primary supporter of Israel
- To abandon Israel and incur the judgment of God prior to the tribulation
- To remain a key player on the world scene, then descend into chaos after the rapture
- To defeat Russia in the Ezekiel 38-39 scenario
- To be destroyed by Russia in the Ezekiel 38-39 scenario
- To be destroyed as prophetical Babylon of Revelation 18
- To be neutralized through terrorism such as an electromagnetic pulse (EMP) attack on our electronic grid
- To experience a financial collapse and go bankrupt as a nation
- To be merged with the EU and become part of a New World Order
- To join with all nations opposing Israel at Armageddon

- Through a combination of all these views seen in light of the entire prophetic scenario

In Revelation 5:8-10 there is a company of people redeemed from every nation kindred and tongue who stand in the presence of God. Historically, the USA church has played a major role in making that happen.

> Although the methods and players have changed, the Evangelical movement has remained constant in the flow of America's religious history. Spreading the Good News will be guaranteed as long as the Constitution's First Amendment continues to be upheld by the U.S. Supreme Court. As stated, "Congress shall make no law respecting an establishment of religion, or prohibiting the free exercise thereof...." With the most recent form of proselytizing on the worldwide web, the effects of that First Amendment guarantee will continue to be felt by those living in the United States as well as around the world.[1]

God's first priority in His kingdom is the proclamation of the gospel. The peace, prosperity, freedom and blessings given to the American church have resulted in the spread of the gospel on a global scale. This is no coincidence, and discerning students of history can clearly see it. Even secular historians have recognized the role evangelism played during the Great Awakening under John Wesley and George Whitefield:

> The Great Awakening was an evangelical movement that had a significant impact on American Protestantism. Its peak period was between the 1730s and 1740s, and it offered people a deep sense of spiritual conviction and redemption by preaching that made faith an intensely personal matter. The Great Awakening was the result of a spiritual dryness among Protestant believers in the Colonies.

One of the biggest effects of the Great Awakening on the Colonies was the way it prepared the people for the War of Independence. The Awakening made the colonists realize that they could have the religious power in their own hands rather than in those of the Church of England. As such, the colonists started to develop a vision of freedom from British rule. The climate created by the Great Awakening made the American Revolution possible. The movement brought religious unity to the colonies, which resulted in political and cultural unity as well. Moreover, this spiritual awakening had a profound impact on the development of the American identity.[2]

Some students of prophecy see a place for the evangelical church to make an impact on world affairs throughout this dispensation of grace. Without any clear indication from scripture to the contrary, we might conclude that the church will continue to evangelize and advance the kingdom of God in whatever time remains in the church age.

Also, as we live in the most prophetic generation in history, it is clear to see that the USA has continued to be a means of support for the modern state of Israel. Yes, there is a fierce conflict between the friends of Israel and the enemies of Israel. Even the church is polarized over the issue of Israel.

Many fundamental, evangelical, dispensational, pentecostal and charismatic believers are firm supporters of the basic right for Israel to exist within safe and secure borders. This belief does not negate the need for individual Jews to know Jesus Christ as personal savior. It does however, encourage Christians to support the fundamental right to existence for the descendants of Abraham, Isaac and Jacob. That very issue will ultimately lead to the battle of Armageddon. America has provided much of that support in the interim between the founding of Israel and the apocalyptic events at the end of the age. Dr. Jerry Falwell listed our support for Israel (Principle of the Abrahamic Covenant) as one of the seven principles which made America great. We hope and pray that remains constant until the end of the age.

An ominous development in USA-Israeli relations which prompted a US House response occurred in the days just preceding the inauguration of Donald Trump as the 45th President of the USA:

> The US House of Representatives passed a scathing rebuke Thursday night to a United Nations Security Council resolution the Obama administration allowed through last month that condemned Israeli settlements as illegal.
>
> House Resolution 11 declared the UN motion a "one-sided" effort that is an obstacle to peace, placing disproportionate blame on Israel for the continuation of the conflict and encouraging Palestinians from engaging in direct, bilateral negotiations.
>
> Passed by a vote of 342-80, the measure puts the lower chamber of Congress firmly against President Barack Obama's decision to withhold the US veto power from shielding Israel against the censure.
>
> UN Resolution 2334 says the settlement enterprise "has no legal validity and constitutes a flagrant violation under international law" and calls for a complete end to all construction in areas Israel captured after the 1967 Six Day War, including East Jerusalem.[3]

The rebuke from the House demonstrates there is a major conflict over the relationship between the USA and Israel. Pundits are suggesting a major change in USA-Israeli relationships now the new administration has taken office. Perhaps, it will lead to a season of greater stability for Israel.

A chaotic scenario may be expected from the rapture of vast numbers of Christians in America:

According to a 2011 Pew Forum study on global Christianity, "285,480,000 or 13.1 percent of all Christians are Evangelicals. The largest concentration of Evangelicals can be found in the United States, with 26.8% of the U.S. population or 94.38 million, the latter being roughly one third of the world's Evangelicals."[4]

Once the rapture transpires Christians will be missing from all walks of life and the USA will be heavily affected. Vice-President Mike Pence is very open about his faith as a born-again Christian; as are believers from every walk of life in America. 94.38 million American Christians will be gone and God only knows the full impact it will have on the USA and other countries.

Dr. Mark Hitchcock has suggested this explanation:

> It appears that in God's timetable, America remains a key player until the Rapture occurs. It's after the Rapture that the Group of Ten come on the scene in Europe, along with the Antichrist, and negotiates the peace treaty that temporarily suspends the Middle East crisis. Up until that point it seems that America will continue to be Israel's key ally and defender. If that's true – if America must remain strong up to the time of the Rapture but afterward be replaced by Europe as the center of power and peace negotiations – then what does all this tell us?
>
> I believe the Rapture will bring America to its knees. The Rapture will change everything. But what is the Rapture? Why will it have such a dramatic effect on geopolitics?"[5]

The instant evacuation of 94.38 million American Christians might explain that.

The late Dr. Hilton Sutton and others have suggested that America may have a major role, if not the leading role in defending Israel from the Russian-Islamic invasion of Israel. These commentators have listed America as part of Tarshish and the Young Lions of Ezekiel 38. However, other commentators only see a diplomatic protest by the Young Lions; while others see a major military conflagration between the USA and Russia there. That passage is clear that Russia is defeated. Whether that comes from military intervention by the USA and her allies or as a sovereign intervention of God is still discussed and debated by serious scholars. Some commentators see a combination of man-made technology such as nuclear weapons as well as sovereign acts of God in fulfillment of these prophecies.

Some commentators suggest that both the USA and Russia are destroyed in this conflagration and the Antichrist moves into the power vacuum left there. If that sounds extreme, keep in mind these battles take place during the last few years of the age leading up to the second coming of Christ. When all the major cities of the world are destroyed it is not difficult to envision such a scenario.

Dr. J. Dwight Pentecost provides a broader perspective on Armageddon in *Things to Come*:

> It has been held commonly that the battle of Armageddon is an isolated event transpiring just prior to the second advent of Christ to the earth. The extent of this great movement in which God deals with "the kings of the earth and of the whole world" (Rev. 16:14) will not be seen unless it is realized that the "battle of that great day of God Almighty" (Rev. 16:14) is not an isolated battle, but rather a campaign that extends over the last half of the tribulation period. The Greek word *polemos*, translated "battle" in Revelation 16:14, signifies a war or campaign, while *machē* signifies a battle, and sometimes even single combat. This distinction is observed by Trench, and is followed by Thayer and Vincent. The use of the world *polemos* (campaign) in Revelation 16:14 would signify that the events that culminate in the gathering at Armageddon at the Second Advent are viewed by God as one connected campaign."[6]

As Pentecost stated, the campaign extends over the last half of the tribulation period, it will be necessary to view and correlate all which transpires during that period to properly interpret how the prophecies will be fulfilled. One should hesitate to be too dogmatic except when necessary for the sake of clear truth.

A number of scholars have suggested the total demise of the USA as prophetical Babylon of Jeremiah 50-51 and Revelation 18, which are tribulation passages. Dr. Jack Van Impe is one of the most prominent proponents of that view:

> There are a number of chapters within God's Word that seem to picture the USA. No other nation throughout history can so convincingly fulfill all of the requirements of the texts. America is certainly included in the judgments upon all nations (Ezekiel 39:21). America also seems to be the political Babylon of Revelation 18. God's Word mentions three Babylons: a city (Genesis 11), a church (Revelation 17), and a country (Revelation 18). Don't confuse the three.
>
> Isaiah, Jeremiah, and John describe this country: Isaiah 18:1, 2 – America's emblem, with outstretched wings, beyond the sea from Israel; a nation, scattered and peeled, meaning spread out and cultured; measured or staked out and polluted in its waterways.
>
> Jeremiah 50 – Here she is called the heritage of the Lord and faces judgment because of her backsliding (vs. 11). A nation of mingled people (vs. 37); a nation whose coexisting "mother" (England) is confounded at the hour of her decline (vs. 12).
>
> Jeremiah 51 – In this text America is bordered by the world's two largest oceans and possesses its longest river (vs. 13); her wealth plagues the nations to jealousy (vs. 7); her space exploits are fantastic (vs. 53).

John picture two Babylons in Revelation. One is a world religion (chapter 17), the other and internationally respected nation (vs. 3); laden with sin (vs. 5), with a superabundance of material goods producing idleness and sin (vs. 7).

America today is surely laden with iniquity with its drunkenness, drug addiction, tobacco, gambling, prostitution, homosexuality, smut peddlers, immorality, abortions, mercy killers, murderers, robbers and looters. There is a specific judgment administered against Babylon, identified as America. A sneak attack is predicted in Jeremiah 50:24 and in one hour, Babylon is destroyed (Revelation 18:10). Some biblical scholars believe that Russia starts the sneak nuclear attack against the USA, crippling her, and then against Israel (Ezekiel 39:2). Whatever the alignment of events, it is clear that both nations fall, Christ returns, and world peace begins."[7]

Many prophecy scholars continue to insist there is no specific mention of the USA in prophecy. One scenario which has been considered adds plausibility to that idea. If the USA were to lose her unique sovereignty as a nation and be merged into a New World Order, she could be allied with the EU or even merged into one of ten global regions proposed by the Club of Rome in 1973. The New World Order is proposed by globalists, including some USA presidents and leading politicians. If the United States were to cede her sovereignty and become part of a global government she might scarcely be recognizable in prophecy. Even with that her wealth and military resources could be utilized to further a globalist agenda. Dr. David Jeremiah included this insight:

America Will Be Incorporated into the European Coalition

Our first answer comes from noted prophecy expert John Walvoord, who wrote:

"Although the Scriptures do not give any clear word concerning the role of the United States in relation to the revived Roman Empire, it is clear this will be a consolidation of the power of the West. Unlike the coalitions led by the United States, this coalition will be led by others—the Group of Ten. . . Most citizens of the United States of America have come from Europe, and their sympathies would more naturally be with a European alliance than with Russia, Asia, and Africa. . . Europe and America may be in formal alliance with Israel in opposition to the radical Islamic countries of the Middle East."[8]

We adapted the following segment from Dr. David Reagan and William Koenig on American presidents earlier in chapter three, emphasizing America's role in bringing Israel into existence. US presidents have interacted both positively and negatively with Israel since 1948:

Harry S. Truman

- First world leader to recognize the state of Israel
- This gave legitimacy to the newborn state
- Referred to it as "the proudest moment of his life"
- Most of his administration opposed it
- However, he instituted an arms embargo on Israel

Dwight D. Eisenhower

- Publicly supported the nation of Israel
- Applied pressure for Israel to withdraw from the Sinai
- First US president to threaten Israel when they hesitated from withdrawal
- He supported a UN resolution condemning them for not withdrawing
- He later expressed regret over having pressured Israel
- He continued the arms embargo instituted by Truman

John F. Kennedy

- Strong supporter of Israel in both word and deed
- He lifted the arms embargo of Truman and Eisenhower
- Extended the first informal security guarantees to Israel in 1962
- Beginning in 1963 he authorized the sale to Israel of advanced US weaponry
- He firmly opposed Israel's development of nuclear weapons
- His brother, Robert F. Kennedy, had pledged to maintain clear and compelling support for Israel
- His assassin, a Palestinian named Sirhan Sirhan said those words led him to kill Bobby

Lyndon B. Johnson

- Johnson was one of the greatest friends of Israel among modern day presidents
- He was often referred to as "America's first Jewish President"
- He worked to establish a refuge in Texas for European Jews fleeing Nazi Germany
- He was deeply influenced by a visit he made to the Dachau death camp in 1945
- Johnson strongly supported Israel during the 1967 Six-day War
- LBJ closely supervised the crafting of UN resolution 242 in 1967 calling for Israel to be guaranteed "secure and recognized boundaries"

Richard M. Nixon

- Nixon is considered today to have been anti-Semitic based on the infamous White House tapes

- He did recognize the importance of the only democratic state in the Middle East
- When Israel was attacked in the 1973 Yom Kippur War he responded with overwhelming aid
- He did that knowing it would alienate the Arab World and the Soviet Union
- Nixon is still admired by the Israelis "as the man who saved Israel"
- Golda Meir never forgot that Israel would have been destroyed if not for Nixon

Gerald R. Ford

- Ford took a hardline stance toward Israel demanding their withdrawal from Sinai which they had recovered during the Yom Kippur War
- Ford's letter to Yitzhak Rabin was harsh and threatening
- Many Senators called on Ford to make it clear that the USA stands firm with Israel
- When the Israelis stalled in response to his demands he froze all scheduled delivery of arms

James Carter

- President Carter put the Sinai issue on the front burner when he came into office
- In 1979, he was able to broker a deal providing a complete withdrawal of Israel from the Sinai Peninsula
- In recent years Carter's writings show him to be a vehement anti-Semite who detests the Israelis
- When the 2014 war between Israel and Hamas broke out, Carter denounced Israel and called for the international recognition of Hamas

Ronald Reagan

- Ronald Reagan has the reputation of being the most pro-Israel president in American history
- Much of that reputation is based on glowing words that he often spoke in support of Israel
- Despite words like this Reagan had a number of run-ins with Israel
- In 1981, he significantly strengthened the Arabs by selling them some of our most sophisticated weapons
- He did that despite great opposition by both the Israelis and the Israeli lobby in Congress
- When Israel bombed the Iraqi nuclear reactor in 1981, Reagan supported the UN Security Council resolution that condemned Israel
- In 1985, Reagan began to provide Israel with $3 billion in foreign aid annually, all in the form of grants
- In 1988, Reagan authorized the State Department to enter dialogue with the PLO, reversing the U.S. policy of refusing to recognize terrorist organizations
- Reagan was infuriated when he was not informed in advance of the Israeli attack on the Iraqi nuclear reactor in 1981, and in that same year, chastised Israel for annexing The Golan Heights
- Menachem Begin accused Reagan of treating Israel like a "banana republic"

George H.W. Bush

- The Bush administration proved to be the decisive turning point in US-Israel relations
- His anti-Semitic Secretary of State, James Baker called for Israel to "abandon its expansionist policies
- Bush announced in 1991 that he considered East Jerusalem to be "occupied territory" despite the fact that Israel had officially annexed it in 1980

- Bush convened an international conference in Madrid, Spain and pursued an Arab-Israeli settlement
- That conference laid the groundwork for the Oslo accords in 1993 initiating the Land-for-Peace process
- Yasser Arafat was invited by James Baker to speak at the Baker Institute for Public Policy at Rice University

William J. Clinton

- Clinton positioned himself as a strong friend of the Jewish people and the nation of Israel
- He provided Israel with substantial financial aid
- He worked constantly behind the scenes to convince Israel to trade land-for-peace
- He presided over the signing of the Oslo accords at the White House in September of 1993
- In 1998, Clinton hosted the Wye River Conference between Arafat and Netanyahu which led to Israel agreeing to withdraw from Hebron
- In 2000, Clinton convened the Camp David Conference between Arafat and Ehud Barak
- Barak offered Arafat all he had ever demanded in diplomatic circles and Arafat walked out, immediately flew back to Israel and launched the Second Intifada
- On October 23, 1995 the US Congress passed the Jerusalem Embassy and Relocation Act
- Clinton refused to sign it and allowed it to become law without his signature

George W. Bush

- George W. Bush vowed not to follow his father's hardline policy toward Israel

- But hardly had he given this assurance, when in 2001, he turned around and called for the establishment of a Palestinian State
- He was the first USA president to do so publicly and formally, proceeding to make it an official part of U.S. foreign policy
- Bush gave new impetus to the Land for Peace strategy by demanding that Israel surrender the Gaza Strip

Barack Obama

- Obama emerged quickly as the most anti-Israel president in U.S. history
- His very first TV interview was granted to the Muslim network, Al Arabiya
- He followed by dashing off to Cairo, Egypt in June 2009 to give his famous apology speech to the Muslim nations of the Middle East
- In July 2009, he announced that the time had come for "daylight" between the United States and Israel
- In May of 2011, the president went on national TV to demand that Israel return to the suicidal borders that existed before the Six Day War in 1967
- In March of 2014, the spokesperson for the State Department announced that the Obama Administration no longer considered it necessary for the Palestinians to recognize the existence of the State of Israel
- Throughout his administration, Obama continued to condemn Israel's settlements as being "illegitimate"
- Obama continued to provide the Palestinian Authority with over $600M in aid each year
- In September of 2012, he proclaimed to the UN in a speech, "The future must not belong to those who slander the prophet of Islam"[9]

Donald J. Trump

- In May of 2017, he became the first President to visit the Western Wall while in office
- On June 6, 2017, the Senate passed a unanimous resolution commemorating the fiftieth anniversary of Israel's reoccupation and unification of Jerusalem in the Six Day War of 1967
- That resolution reaffirmed the Jerusalem Embassy Act of 1995, recognizing Jerusalem as the capital of the State of Israel, with the US Embassy located there
- President Trump made his proclamation to move the embassy on December 6, 2017
- Trump has assembled the most formidable Foreign Policy team in history
- Trump: Israel will pay a 'higher price' in peace talks after embassy move
- US, Israel officials downplay Trump's warning of 'price' over Jerusalem moves
- Trump endorses separate Palestinian state as goal of Mideast peace talks
- U.S. expects some Israeli criticism on coming Mideast plan
- Trump has the most formidable M.E. team in history
- Pence: Trump, greatest defender Israel ever had in WH!
- USA is entering an era of economic growth and prosperity greater than we have seen in decades.
- Election of Trump gives a window of opportunity to the church![10]

Summary of the USA in Prophecy

Ultimately, all the nations of the world will march to Israel at the end of Daniel's Seventieth Week. This may include the geographical territory of the USA in whatever form of government exists at that time. The book of Revelation makes it clear that all the major cities of the world will be destroyed and apart from God's divine intervention no flesh would be left alive on planet earth. God will intervene!

> Scripturally we attribute the events of the tribulation period to the Day of the Lord, a theme repeated throughout the scriptures. You and I as New Testament believers are not a part of that prophetic scenario in which God deals more openly in the affairs of men. Although we see that prophetic scenario coming into focus now, we will not be here when God's wrath is poured out. Yes, we could experience persecution, some loss of freedom, prosperity and material blessings, but not the wrath of God. We might conclude that the USA will continue as a major player in world evangelism and teaching ministry to the nations up until the tribulation, although we wouldn't be dogmatic.

> Dr. Tim LaHaye once asked, "Does there have to be a tribulation before the tribulation?" If Christians abandon their biblical and civic responsibilities, we will suffer things that may otherwise have been avoided. In 1979, Dr. LaHaye, Dr. Jerry Falwell and others helped found the Moral Majority and led a generation of born-again Christians to get involved in helping to return our country to "The Seven Principles that made America Great." Ever since that time, there has been an evangelical voice in American politics. Politicians have factored that into their campaigns as they appeal for support from Christians. It was a pivotal time in American history and its effects are still being felt today:

> In the last election [millions of] evangelical Christians stayed home. If Christians will simply show up and vote our values, we'll turn this nation around" – Senator Ted Cruz [11]

American support for Israel has been evident for decades. There is major pressure on world leaders over the handling of the Middle East crisis. The Obama administration turned as sharply against Israel as any American president ever had. President Trump has begun with one of the strongest pro-Israeli positions of any US administration in decades. However, if he were to continue the pattern of forcing land for peace on Israel as past administrations have done, the USA will experience judgments in some form from God.

If the USA loses her unique sovereignty and is merged into a New World Order, she would scarcely resemble what she did in the generation following WWII. Many world leaders and elected USA officials have been working against national sovereignty for decades. With the absence of millions of born-again Christians, there would be little if any salt and light to preserve the downward spiral of this nation. The final scenario would fall into place quickly and global chaos would surely ensue at that time. Ultimately all the nations of the world will march on Israel and at that time America will not have enough moral and spiritual strength to avoid becoming a part of that scenario. Without the influence of Bible believing Christians "The Seven Principles that made America Great" would fall by the wayside rapidly.

Chapter 9

Convergence: Bringing the Signs of the Times into Focus

We have documented a wide array of scriptural events all of which began to be fulfilled concurrently in this generation. Seen individually, they may not be of much significance, but seen as a comprehensive worldview they offer compelling evidence that we are living in the last days and the stage is being set for Daniel's Seventieth Week.

A prophesied series of events have appeared for the first time in human history as documented in chapter two. They are repeated here for emphasis in our conclusion.

For the first time in history, man has the capacity to:

- Destroy all life on planet Earth (Matt. 24:21-22)
- Destroy one half of humanity in the tribulation (Rev. 6:8; 9:15)
- Burn one-third of the earth by fire (Rev. 9:18)
- Generate 100-pound hailstones with nuclear weapons (Rev. 16:21)
- Cause human flesh to melt from the body instantly (Zech. 14:12)
- Number and track the buying and selling of all mankind (Rev.13:16-18)
- Address all mankind and broadcast any event to a global audience (Rev. 11:7-12)

Certain key events are predicted for the last days:

- The Information Age: an increase in knowledge and travel (Dan. 12:4)
- Widespread persecution and martyrdom of Christians (Matt. 10:22; Rev. 6:9)
- A revival of ancient occultism and eastern mysticism (Matt. 24:5)
- A widespread interest in UFOs and extraterrestrial beings (2 Thess. 2:11-12)

- A global outpouring of The Holy Spirit with preaching of the Gospel (Acts 2:16-18)
- The rise of many false Christs and false prophets who work miracles (Matt. 24:5)
- Rejection of biblical authority and doctrine by false church leaders (1 Tim. 4:1; Rev. 17)
- Many depart from the faith and give heed to seducing spirits (1 Tim. 4:1-6)
- An ecumenical movement emerges uniting all religions into a false church (Rev. 17)
- Widespread unbelief in the Rapture and the Second Coming of Christ (2 Pet. 3:3-4)

The nations of the world aligned in Bible prophecy:

- Israel is restored as a nation after a 2000-year dispersion (Ezek. 37:39)
- Jerusalem becomes a burdensome political problem to world leaders (Zech. 12:3)
- The Arab-Israeli conflict over land and the city of Jerusalem (Gen. 17:20-21; Rev. 6-19)
- Europe is united as a superpower with a movement for world government (Dan. 2:37-44)
- There is a call for one man to lead the entire world (Rev. 13:8)
- Hatred of the Islamic nations for the reborn state of Israel (Gen. 16:11-13)
- Russia and her Islamic allies invade Israel during the tribulation period (Ezek. 1 38-39)
- China and her Oriental allies move into the Middle East (Rev.16:12-14)
- The USA and her allies are drawn into the Arab-Israeli conflict (Ezek. 38-39; Rev. 6-19)
- The Arab-Israeli conflict involves all the nations of the world (Ezek. 38-39; Rev. 6-19)

- Armageddon threatens the survival of the human race (Matt. 24:21-22)
- The return of Christ to Earth saves mankind from complete annihilation (Rev. 19:11-16)

Once Jesus Christ returns and the unbelieving world is left behind, the horrors of the tribulation period will unfold. The nations of the world will be battling for global dominance and most prophecy scholars believe all out nuclear war will take place. Many of the judgments described in the book of Revelation could be created with modern technology. God sovereignly guides the flow of history and it appears that a grand climax is approaching within our time. These spheres of geopolitical power dominate the news today; Israel, the Islamic nations, Russia, China, the USA and Europe as well. Antichrist will arise to power after the church is gone.

Throughout this book, I have carefully documented numerous sources that these events were prophesied in scripture centuries ago and are being fulfilled in the news events of today. It is unreasonable to assume that these have simply happened by random chance. It is much easier to believe that the author of Scripture knew the end from the beginning and is providentially guiding the flow of history. Yes, that involves faith in a supernatural, sovereign God Who works all things after the counsel of His divine will; and faith is easier than unbelief. Those who deliberately choose to suppress the truth and reject the Word of God will be held accountable and be without excuse on judgment day. Those who receive Jesus Christ as personal Lord and Savior will spend eternity with Him in heaven.

If you have been made to see the reality of scripture and your need of Jesus Christ, He is knocking at the door of your heart. You can repent of your sins and trust His shed blood as the payment for your sins. Simply repeating a prayer without faith or sincerity will not save you, but if you will come to Christ in repentance and faith He will receive you.

You can pray like this*:*

Dear God,

I am a lost sinner. I repent of my sins. I believe that Christ died for me and was raised from the dead. I trust in His precious blood. Lord Jesus Christ, come into my heart and save me now, and I thank you it is done.

Amen.

If you prayed to receive Christ and meant it, you are saved on the authority of the written Word of God (Romans 10:13).

Find a strong Bible believing church and begin to fulfill God's plan and purpose for your life.

1) Be baptized (immersed) in water (Matthew 28:19-20)

2) Be filled with the Holy Spirit (Acts 1:8; 2:4; 8:14-17)

3) Join a church which teaches the verbal inspiration and inerrancy of the Bible (66 books), the Trinity, the Deity and Virgin Birth of Christ, salvation by repentance and faith in Christ's shed blood, the new birth, holy living, Christ's bodily resurrection and His literal second coming (Jude 3)

4) Read and study the scriptures systematically (2 Timothy 2:15)

5) Spend time in prayer daily (Luke 18:1; Ephesians 6:18)

6) Confess your sins to God (1 John 1:9)

7) Jesus said, "Whosoever therefore shall confess me before men, him will I confess also before my Father which is in heaven." (Matthew 10:32)

Please contact us at the ministry as we have resources to strengthen you in your walk with Him. The ministry website is found at **www.awmin.org.** Grace and Peace to You!

About the Author

Dr. Allan Walker travels as an Evangelist, Bible Teacher and Singer in churches and conferences. He was ordained into the ministry in 1980 and has worked in all facets of local church ministry, serving as pastor, associate pastor, children's pastor, worship leader and board member. He also served on staff with The Voice of the Martyrs for sixteen years. He is ordained through the Independent Assemblies Fellowship. Allan has a Ph.D. in Biblical Prophecy from Christ's College in Cocoa, FL. He has ministered in numerous local churches and seminars across the country and has been a guest on radio and TV broadcasts. He has given presentations on the persecuted church at Christ for the Nations in Dallas, TX. He has done teaching and evangelism in both Honduras and Chiapas, Mexico.

Allan has been a guest of Dr. David Reagan on Lamb and Lion's weekly television program called "Christ in Prophecy." This program is broadcast nationally on six Christian networks which combined have access to 109 million homes in America. And through the satellite systems of some of these networks, they have access to every nation in the world. The program deals with the prophetic significance of national and international events.

Allan has been a repeat guest of Dr. Hormoz Shariat on the Iran Alive Broadcast where over 55 million Iranians have access to satellite TV. Bestselling author, Joel Rosenberg has referred to Dr. Shariat as "The Billy Graham of Iran." At any given time, 3-6 million viewers will be watching the programs. Their satellite footprint reaches the Middle East, North Africa, and Europe.

Allan is a member of the Pre-Trib Study Group founded by Dr. Tim LaHaye. He has been a speaker and provided music for the Mid-America Prophecy Conference in Tulsa, OK. He gives presentations on Bible Prophecy 101, The Tabernacle, The Holy Spirit and a number of other biblical topics important in ministry.

He is open for church meetings and conferences throughout the USA. Free study resources are available on the multimedia page of our website. The ministry website is found at www.awmin.org or call 918-559-5200.

Bibliography

Chapter 1. The Divine Design of Bible Prophecy

[1] Pentecost, J. Dwight. *Things to Come.* Thomas Nelson. 1958. Used with permission of Thomas Nelson. www.thomasnelson.com.

[2] Lindsey, Hal. raptureready.com/who/Hal_Lindsey.html Date of Access. Dec. 11, 2016

[3] Tim LaHaye Ministries. timlahaye.com Date of Access. Dec. 11, 2016

[4] "Clarence Larkin." en.wikipedia.org/wiki/Clarence_Larkin Date of Access Dec. 11, 2016.

[5] Pentecost, J. Dwight. *Things to Come.* Thomas Nelson. 1958. Used with permission of Thomas Nelson. www.thomasnelson.com.

Chapter 2. Sign One: Ancient Prophecies Coming into Focus

[1] Industry Tap. www.industrytap.com/knowledge-doubling-every-12-months-soon-to-be-every-12-hours/3950 Date of Access, Nov. 22, 2016

[2] CNS News. www.cnsnews.com/news/article/lauretta-brown/ Date of Access, Nov. 22, 2016

[3] His Heavenly Armies. hisheavenlyarmies.com/reasons-for-the-modern-occult-revival/ Date of Access, Nov. 22, 2016

[4] The Truth Wins. thetruthwins.com/archives/more-americans-believe-aliens-have-visited-earth-than-believe-that-jesus-is-the-son-of-god Date of Access, Nov. 22, 2016

[5] Assemblies of God. www.holyspirit.ag.org/spirit.html Date of Access, Nov. 22, 2016

[6] "Charismatic Christianity." en.wikipedia.org/wiki/Charismatic_Christianity Date of Access, Nov. 22, 2016

[7] Hartford Institute. hirr.hartsem.edu/research/quick_question41.html Date of Access, Dec. 16, 2016

[8] Pew Forum. "Global Christianity." www.pewforum.org/2011/12/19/global-christianity-exec/ Date of Access, Jan. 8, 2017

[9] Davis, A.A. *The Trail of Blood.* 1952.

[10] One News Now. "Evangelicals Infected with Inclusivism." www.onenewsnow.com/church/2016/01/22/jeffress-evangelicals-infected-with-inclusivism Date of Access, Nov. 25, 2016

[11] D.U.O. "7 Principles." www.dountoothers.org/7principles.html, Date of Access, Dec. 13, 2016

[12] Berkley Center. "Ghandi on Unity of All Religions." berkleycenter.georgetown.edu/quotes/mohandas-gandhi-on-the-unity-of-all-religions Date of Access, Nov. 25, 2016

[13] Lamb and Lion Ministries. "Apostasy in the Church." christinprophecy.org/articles/apostasy-in-the-church/ Date of Access, Nov. 25, 2016

[14] Amazing Discoveries. "Pope Francis Urges All Religions to Unite." amazingdiscoveries.org/13.04.29-pope-francis-now-urges-all-religions-to-unite Date of Access, Nov.25, 2016

[15] Wright. N.T. "Farewell to the Rapture." ntwrightpage.com/2016/07/12/farewell-to-the-rapture/ Date of Access, Nov. 25, 2016

[16] "50 Reasons." www.lamblion.com/xfiles/publications/magazines/Lamplighter_JanFeb08_50Reasons.pdf. Date of Access, Dec. 23, 2016.

Chapter 3

Sign Two: Israel – The Super Sign of Prophecy

[1] Jeremiah, David. *What in the World is Going On?* Thomas Nelson, 2008. Used with permission of Thomas Nelson. www.thomasnelson.com.

[2] "Judaism Revolt" www.jewishvirtuallibrary.org/jsource/Judaism/revolt.html, Date of Access, Dec. 11, 2016

[3] Davis, A.A. *The Trail of Blood.* 1952.

[4] Adapted-Lamplighter Magazine Jan/Feb 2015, www.lamblion.com, Used by permission.

[5] Adapted-Lamplighter Magazine, March/April, July/August 2018 www.lamblion.com, and Koenig World Watch Daily, www.watch.org, Used by permission.

[6] Anderson, Robert. *The Coming Prince.* 14th ed., Grand Rapids, MI. Kregal Publications, 1957. Used by permission of the publisher.

[7] "Isaac Newton." www.pretribulation.com/isaac-newton.htm, Date of Access, Dec. 11, 2016

[8] "History of Crucifixion and Archeological Proof of the Cross, as Opposed to a Stake." www.bible.ca/d-history-archeology-crucifixion-cross.htm, Date of Access, Dec 15, 2016

[9] CBN. "Psalm 22 and Passion of Jesus." www1.cbn.com/psalm-22-and-passion-jesus Date of Access, Dec. 26, 2016

[10] Rhodes, Ron. *The Popular Dictionary of Bible Prophecy.* Harvest House, 2010.

[11] Christians United for Israel. *Israel 101 e-book.* San Antonio.

[12] Lamplighter Magazine, Jan/Feb 2015, www.lamblion.com, Used with permission.

Chapter 4

Sign Three: The Arab-Israeli Conflict

[1] Lamb and Lion Ministries. "Arabs." www.lamblion.com/xfiles/publications/magazines/Lamplighter_NovDec02_Arabs.pdf. Date of Access, Dec. 23, 2016

[2] Lamb and Lion Ministries. "Middle East Crisis" www.lamblion.com/xfiles/publications/magazines/Lamplighter_Jul Aug02_MiddleEastCrisis.pdf. Date of Access, Dec. 23, 2016

[3] "Arab World." en.wikipedia.org/wiki/Arab_world Date of Access, Dec.23, 2016

[4] "Israeli Settlement." en.wikipedia.org/wiki/Israeli_settlement, Date of Access, Dec. 23, 2016

[5] Lamb and Lion Ministries. "Middle East Crisis." www.lamblion.com/xfiles/publications/magazines/Lamplighter_Jul Aug02_MiddleEastCrisis.pdf. December 23, 2016

[6] Shahid, Dr. Samuel. *The Last Trumpet: A Comparative Study in Christian-Islamic Eschatology.* Xulon Press, 2005.

[7] Lamb and Lion Ministries. "Islam Eschatology" www.lamblion.com/xfiles/publications/magazines/Lamplighter_M ayJun06_IslamEschatology.pdf. Date of Access, Dec. 23, 2016

[8] Pre-Trib Research Center. "Battle of Gog and Magog." pre-trib.org/articles/view/battle-of-gog-and-magog, Date of Access, Dec. 26, 2016

Chapter 5

Sign Four: Russia, Gog, Magog and the Middle East

[1] "Cold War." en.wikipedia.org/wiki/Cold_War Date of Access, Dec. 26, 2016

---

[2] Pre-Trib Research Center. "Ezekiel 38-39." pre-trib.org/articles/view/ezekiel-38-39-part-2, Segments 2-9, Date of Access, Dec. 30, 2016

Chapter 6

Sign Five: Antichrist, EU and the New World Order

[1] Pre-Trib Research Center. "Israel and European Union." pre-trib.org/articles/view/israel-and-european-union Date of Access, Jan. 2, 2017

[2] Pre-Trib Research Center. "Brexit and the European Union." pre-trib.org/articles/view/brexit-and-the-european-union Date of Access, Jan. 2, 2017

Chapter 7

Sign Six: China, the Kings of the East and Armageddon

[1] Pre-Trib Research Center. "Prophetic Significance of Rise of China." pre-trib.org/articles/view/prophetic-significance-of-rise-china-as-world-power, Date of Access, Jan. 2, 2017

[2] Koinonia House. "Strategic Trends – China." www.khouse.org/strategic_trends/china/full_details/ Date of Access, January 2, 2017

Chapter 8

Sign Seven: The USA, Jerusalem and the Middle East

[1] U.S. History. www.u-s-history.com/pages/h3817.html Date of Access, Jan. 7, 2017

[2] "Did Great Awakening Affect Colonies?" www.reference.com/history/did-great-awakening-affect-colonies-f1999a5f7c928c0f Date of Access, Jan. 7, 2017

[3] Koenig's World News. www.watch.org Date of Access, Jan. 7, 2017

[4] Pew Forum. "Global Christianity Regions." www.pewforum.org/2011/12/19/global-christianity-regions/

[5] Hitchcock, Dr. Mark. *The Late Great United States.* Colorado Springs, Multnomah, 2009.

[6] Pentecost, J. Dwight. *Things to Come.* Thomas Nelson. 1958. Used with permission of Thomas Nelson. www.thomasnelson.com.

[7] Van Impe, Dr. Jack. *The Jack Van Impe Prophecy Bible.* 1999.

[8] Jeremiah, David. *What in the World is Going On?* Thomas Nelson, 2008. Used with permission of Thomas Nelson. www.thomasnelson.com.

[9] Adapted-Lamplighter Magazine Jan/Feb 2015, www.lamblion.com, Used by permission

[10] Adapted-Lamplighter Magazine, March/April, July/August 2018 www.lamblion.com, and Koenig World Watch Daily, www.watch.org, Used by permission.

[11] "Hey Conservative Post" www.facebook.com/heyconservativepost/ Date of Access, Sept. 21, 2015

24130871R00078

Made in the USA
San Bernardino, CA
03 February 2019